HEALTHFUL TRAVEL

Your Peace-of-Mind Traveling Companion

By Marlene Coleman, M. D.

Healthful Travel

Your Peace-of-Mind Traveling Companion

By Marlene Coleman, M.D.

Published by:
International Challenge Publishing Company
800 West First Street, Suite 708
Los Angeles, California 90012

Copyright © 1995 by Marlene Coleman, M.D.

Printed in the United States of America
First Edition 1995

Library of Congress Catalog Number: 94-96621

ISBN: 0-9641050-0-4

Cover and book design by One-On-One Book Production, West Hills, California

To Bill with love...
for your sense of humor...for past and future
healthful travel together.

ABOUT THE AUTHOR

Marlene Coleman, M. D. has a special interest in travel medicine. She is an attending physician at the Caltech Health Center and helps to keep students healthy as they study, lecture and travel all over the world. Dr. Coleman is also a Captain in the United States Naval Reserve Medical Corps and served in Operation Desert Storm.

She is an Associate Clinical Professor of Family Medicine at the University of Southern California Medical School and she maintains a private practice promoting healthful travel. Dr. Coleman is an active member of ZONTA International and served as President of its Pasadena, California chapter. She is also a member of the American Association of Tropical Medicine and Hygiene.

ACKNOWLEDGMENTS

Information obtained from health care and travel authorities has been incorporated in *Healthy Travel* and I would like to thank the following people for their contributions.

My appreciation goes to my family, colleagues and friends who love traveling and have given me invaluable information for this book and have encouraged me to write it.

I especially wish to thank Dr. Darlene Duncan whose contribution as a clinical psychologist has been priceless; Carolyn Porter and Alan Gadney from One-on-One Book Production and Marketing; Barbara Riley for her early morning and late night transcriptions; my colleagues at Caltech, especially Marie Robles; Second Careers; Barbara Swain for·her enthusiasm; and Lou Hoover , who has helped me greatly in taking care of details.

Table of Contents

Suggestions for Specific Travelers

Appendix

INTRODUCTION

A mong the many things we can do to relieve stress and recharge ourselves is to take a relaxing, educational, or inspiring trip. Travel can be necessary for our psychological well-being, but a trip that's marred by illness, poor planning, or lack of preparedness to deal with emergencies can actually create anxiety and stress.

This book will help to prepare you for healthful and happy travel and for any unexpected challenges that might occur. You can take it with you on your travels and have ready answers for most health-related questions and references to health-care facilities in case of emergencies.

Whether you are taking a two-hour automobile trip, an around-the-world flight, or a cruise, my aim is to help you confront problems that can occur with vital information to meet your needs.

TRAVEL TIPS FOR EVERYONE

Healthful Travel includes:

- Preparing for a successful trip
- Problems and illnesses any traveler may encounter
- Traveling with your children
- Traveling by yourself
- Traveling for business
- Traveling with existing medical conditions
- Traveling with physical handicaps
- Traveling for the elderly
- Traveling while pregnant

BEFORE YOU GO ANYWHERE . . .

Here are some IMPORTANT QUESTIONS to ask yourself:

- How do you feel about traveling? What are your limitations?
- Do you know the climate where you're going and whether you can tolerate it?
- What modes of travel are available to take you to your destination, and which do you prefer?
- What is the best kind of trip for you? Long or short, local or international?
- Have you made a budget for yourself? Is it realistic?
- Who is a compatible traveling companion?
- What should you take with you, and how should you carry it?
- Have you made plans to take care of what you will leave behind?

If you're realistic about your travel requirements and expectations, and if you follow the suggestions in this book, you're sure to enjoy yourself!

ADDITIONAL RESOURCES

Because this book should travel with you, I have included many important addresses and contacts in the Appendix, which should help you you to find information to locate doctors, clinics, hospitals in many countries as well as other pertinent travel information.

Wherever you are, wherever you go, this book will be your passport to healthy traveling and peace of mind.

MYTHS ABOUT TRAVEL

Y ou may be surprised to learn that common assumptions about travel are not always true. Here are some things to consider before making any reservations or deposits. This list may help you make very important vacation decisions.

Myth #1: *A vacation is a cure for depression.*

Depression can be deepened while one is surrounded by happy people. Seeking the cause of depression is far more important than masking it with artificial good times.

Myth #2: *Vacations usually help couples to get closer together.*

Vacations sometimes increase stress because couples are together for longer periods of time than under normal circumstances.

Myth #3: *Hard-driving high achievers are always great traveling companions.*

They are often compulsive workers, and time spent away from work could create anxiety for them. They may set strenuous itineraries and goals. They can be insufferably bossy.

Myth #4: *People who don't want to travel usually enjoy it once they are on vacation.*

If your spouse or partner is a homebody, you may be better off with separate vacation time so that you can satisfy your individual needs and wants.

Myth #5: *Children enjoy traveling as much as or more than adults.*

Ordinarily children are not the best traveling companions. They may enjoy a holiday away from home, but they should not be required to sit for long periods in automobiles, theaters, buses, restaurants, or other confined places. Their sight-seeing should be kept to a minimum.

Myth #6: *There is no way to tell if someone will be a good traveling companion.*

A short camping trip is a good test. Any observation on how people handle stress, however small, will give you a good idea about how well you will travel together.

TRAVELING TOGETHER HAPPILY

Travel often brings out the best and the worst in us. It creates a hothouse environment in which relationships either grow or spoil. People who travel with their best friends may never speak to them again; others develop a deep and abiding relationship with people they barely knew before. Why does this happen?

Primarily it has to do with the fact that we are all different, and some of these differences are major. No matter how well we think we know another person, living together in the forced closeness of travel accentuates differences we never paid much attention to before. The question is not how different we are, but how well we tolerate those differences in each other.

It comes down to a matter of respect—for ourselves and for others. We all have different needs, ideas, standards, and habits that we have gotten comfortable with, and we all have developed varying degrees of tolerance for those who differ from us. Here are some important points to consider when you decide to travel with another person.

1. **Leaders and followers.** Perhaps one member of the party will take the responsibility to be the leader. This only works when the other members agree to be the followers. Some people might prefer, in the interest of harmony and to avoid a confrontation, to try to "go along." Another may actually enjoy having someone else make all the decisions—or may build resentment that either turns into misery or finally explodes into anger. Discuss and agree beforehand on the degree of leadership that would be acceptable to everyone.

2. **Get to know your roommate.** Beware of roommates you don't know well. On a recent tour, to save money, an older woman accepted as her roommate another older woman, who, she discovered, was making her last trip before becoming totally disabled by a progressive cancer. Unfortunately, she was already sick and required an inordinate amount of care from her roommate until she finally left the tour to return home. Another had a roommate who spent a full hour in the bathroom each morning. Decide what you will tolerate and also consider if you can be with people who smoke or snore.

3. **Talkers and listeners.** Some people like to talk and require the give-and-take of conversation; others don't like to talk very much, or need a lot of attentive listening to be able to talk. Some people like to do all the talking. The wrong mix can be deadly on a long trip.

4. **Politics and religion.** Everyone has an opinion about these subjects, and some feel more strongly about them than others. Unless you can agree to share or withhold your opinions, you may not be able to enjoy yourself.

5. **Personal space.** People have different needs for closeness or distance. A trip puts people very close for a long time. After a while, each may benefit from a day or an excursion away from the other, and at the end of the separation each will be glad to see the other again.

6. **Know your emotional boundaries.** Some people have tough, impermeable boundaries that protect them from hurt but make it hard for others to touch them. Others have soft, permeable boundaries, are easily hurt, and need a lot of care and consideration. Some people are rough and abrasive; others are carefully respectful of boundaries, their own and others; some nice but unassertive people invite others to take advantage of them and yet resent it.

7. **Living up to expectations.** We all have expectations of others—how they should be, how they should act, how we think they are. On a long trip we are likely to discover that our expectations were wrong; people are likely to be different from what we thought they were. It is at this point that relationships are made or broken. If we can find the differences not only acceptable, but interesting and likable, and so adjust our expectations toward reality, we are likely to have a better and more solidly based relationship.

PERSONAL NOTES AND REMINDERS

TRAVEL PREPARATION

PRE-TRIP PREPARATION

PLAN AHEAD—The more you know and prepare for a healthful trip before you leave, the more likely you are to have a great time. Start with a good travel agent/travel counselor:

❖ Word of mouth is one of the best ways of obtaining a good travel agent. It is a good idea to develop a personal relationship with a travel agent so that he/she knows your likes, dislikes, budget, and general personality.

❖ Make sure the travel agent is certified. The agent's business card should have "C.T.C." on it. This means the person completed a certified course and has at least five years of experience as a travel agent. Also make sure the agent uses a computer for booking.

❖ Learn as much as you can about the places where you'll be going by studying brochures. Prepare yourself before taking up a travel agent's time.

❖ Try to choose an agent who is familiar with the area you wish to visit. Obtain current maps of the cities where you will be staying and study them.

On The Way

❖ When flying to your destination, fly nonstop, if possible, to minimize fatigue and tiredness. Think of your own rhythms.

❖ You should take 1-2 days rest for each time zone change and not be on a whirlwind tour to see it all this trip. Take time to adjust to a new destination.

❖ When flying, dehydration is common. Don't forget to increase water consumption in moderation just before and during your flight and remember to walk around every so often during the flight (see the exercises on pages 26 and 27).

MAINTAIN YOUR HEALTH

1. **Know where you can get medical help.** If you have a chronic illness, choose locations to visit where you can get access to health care to keep you active on your trip.

   You can obtain a list of English-speaking physicians in the countries you plan to visit before you leave. The list is available through U.S. consulates or the International Association for Medical Assistance to Travelers (IAMAT), 417 Center Street, Lewiston, NY 14092, (716) 754-4883 (find more information about IAMAT in Appendix).

2. **Be aware of immunization requirements.** If you're traveling to countries outside the "developed" world, ask your physician several months ahead of time what immunization shots you will need. Some immunizations require more than one or two shots to be fully effective.

   There are an increasing number of physicians who specialize in giving immunizations and travel counseling. Medical clinics throughout the United States that have an interest in this specialty are listed in the Appendix.

3. **Be knowledgeable about the climate.** When choosing a vacation, climate can make the difference between a good or a bad time. If you dislike either extreme hot or cold, bear in mind that summertime in the northern hemisphere is wintertime in the southern hemisphere.

4. **Time zones can have an effect on you.** A few comments are included in the chapter on Jet Lag, as well as additional resources in the Appendix.

5. **Illness from eating or drinking in foreign countries can be dangerous.** Travelers who eat from street-vending carts in tropical cities usually become ill, and some have

even died. Stick to bottled water or other bottled beverages.

6. **Decide to have fun and remain calm.** Frustrations are bound to occur, with unexpected events that can lead to stress, so try to be patient.

MORE ABOUT PROTECTION FROM INFECTIOUS DISEASES

It is difficult for embassies and consulates in the United States to keep abreast of vaccination requirements for certain countries, or to find health professionals who are knowledgeable about giving information to travelers. Therefore, it is more important to use your own good judgment in obtaining the best advice. The Appendix information will help you contact some appropriate, knowledgeable physicians and staff who are interested in travel medicine and who update their knowledge frequently.

Adults commonly forget that they as well as their their children must be properly immunized. When planning a trip, check at least two or three months ahead of time to be sure that your immunizations are up-to-date. Children are usually more likely to be current on their immunizations than most adults because of routine scheduling and requirements by most schools.

❖ Find out what diseases are prevelant in the countries where you will be traveling and get good advice about protection.

❖ Adults may not be aware that diphtheria immunizations should be repeated every 10 years. Increased reports of diphtheria have especially surfaced in Russia, where fewer people are being vaccinated.

❖ Malaria does kill, but it can start as a subtle disease, beginning with flu-like symptons after one arrives home. It is important to check with a physician knowledgeable about countries with malaria, and learn of the current medicine recommended. *Remember that malaria medica-*

tions are taken prior to travel, and continued after returning home.

❖ Use caution when taking malaria drugs if you are taking quinine, beta blockers, calcium channel antagonists, or any other types of drugs that can affect a cardiac condition.

❖ It is also important to know that pregnant women should not take certain anti-malaria medications. Also small children and individuals with psychological problems should avoid certain medications.

❖ Gamma globulin is helpful in preventing hepatitis A, but it is believed to be effective for only 5-6 months. Gamma globulin is most effective when given as close to travel departure as possible. *Hepatitis A vaccine is available in some European countries but not yet available in the United States.*

❖ Check with informative sources, such as the public health services and travel clinics, as well as knowledgeable physicians, regarding vaccinations required for diseases such as yellow fever, typhoid, and cholera in certain countries you might be planning to visit.

Additional immunizations, such as influenza vaccine and pneumococeal vaccine, may also be recommended for older travelers and people with high-risk medical conditions. *Check with your physician.*

For a current directory of traveler's health and tropical medicine physicians, mainly in the United States and Canada, send a 9" x 11" stamped, self-addressed envelope to: **Dr. Leonard C. Marcus, 148 Highland Ave., Newton, MA 02165.**

Tips For Choosing A Medical Travel Clinic

❖ Choose a clinic associated with a medical school, university or respected hospital.

❖ Choose a physician or a clinic with a good reputation

13

among experienced travelers in your area. (Ask a travel agent whom you respect.)

❖ Choose a physician specializing in emporiatrics or travel medicine. (Ask local medical schools.)

❖ Choose a physician with membership in the Amercian Society of Tropical Medicine and Hygiene. They most likely would have a good interest in travel medicine.

CHECK YOUR HEALTH INSURANCE

Is your health care coverage sufficient for traveling? Whether you plan to travel internationally or domestically, this is a good question to ask your insurance agent. Call your agent before your departure and see if you need to purchase supplemental insurance.

Medicare generally does not pay for hospital or medical services outside the United States; however, if you're going to the U.S. territories of Puerto Rico, the U.S. Virgin Islands, Guam, American Samoa, and the Northern Marianas, you may be covered. Medicare may pay some benefits in rare cases for emergency care in Canada or Mexico. Check to see if you have coverage before you leave .

To fill insurance coverage gaps for travel outside the United States, you might consider enrolling in a supplemental short-term health policy offered by some companies. A range of options is available, including coverage for health care, assistance in finding a physician or hospital, assistance in contacting your personal physician, and medical transportation abroad or home. Some companies also include benefits for baggage delay or loss, trip cancellation, and legal assistance. Costs vary depending on coverage and the length of the trip. Companies offering this short-term travel insurance are listed in the Appendix.

MORE HELPFUL TIPS

Here are some additional measures that will help you during your vacation:

❖ Take extra blank claim forms.

❖ Satisfy routine health needs before leaving home. For example, if you need periodic bloodpressure monitoring, schedule a visit before you leave.

❖ Learn important phrases and words that will facilitate your stay in a foreign country.

❖ Pay in advance for tours and services when possible. Carry vouchers for services to limit the amount of money you have to carry.

❖ Memorize your passport number and take photo copies of your passport in case it is lost or stolen.

The Citizen's Emergency Center of the Bureau of Consumer Affairs maintains a telephone hotline, (202) 647-5225 from 8:30 a.m. to 10:00 p.m. (EST) Monday through Friday. They can give you the latest information on safety conditions in any part of the world.

KEEP HOME AND HEARTH SAFE

Now that you've made your plans, follow the suggested checklist to make sure your home is safe while you're gone.

❖ Stop mail and newspaper delivery.

❖ Be sure to plan for the care and feeding of pets. Prepare for any other pet needs, such as whom to call in an emergency.

❖ Lock valuables in a safe place, such as a safe deposit box.

❖ Lock all doors, windows, and sliding glass doors.

❖ Turn off and unplug all appliances, such as irons, stoves, and coffee makers.

❖ Turn off outside water faucets and hoses.

❖ Turn off all lights. Some people attach a timer to a single light indoors so that the house does not appear vacant.

Thieves know that porch lights that are left on during the daytime are an invitation to steal.

❖ Check alarm system to be sure it is functioning properly.

❖ Leave your itinerary with a neighbor or relative in case emergencies occur.

❖ Choose someone to watch and check your house frequently to give you peace of mind while you are traveling.

LUGGAGE SUGGESTIONS

Choose well-made, lightweight luggage with sturdy locks. Place identification on both the outside and inside, using a business address, if possible. Believe it or not, choosing the right luggage can help prevent back problems. Several small pieces of luggage are much better than one or two unwieldy, large pieces.

❖ When traveling by air, always take carry-on luggage containing important personal items, especially medications, extra eye glasses, or contacts.

❖ There may not be porters everywhere you go, so travel as efficiently as possible and strive to take luggage that you can carry yourself.

Shoulder Bags are advisable to use, but remember to give your shoulders a rest. Don't use just one shoulder to carry the bag; shift from shoulder to shoulder. This will prevent a constant heavy weight on one side that could result in shoulder or back pain. Two small shoulder bags are ideal for some travelers.

It is tempting to use suitcases **with wheels**, particularly very large ones, because of the perception that you can carry more if you can roll it along. However, these large bags with wheels have a tendency to fall over frequently, and if a wheel breaks, you have a large, heavy suitcase to lug around.

Some travelers prefer to use the **fold-up pull-carts** that enable you to carry heavy loads easily. Try to check them out first to see that the handles are at a proper height for you and that the wheels go up and down stairs easily.

A WORD ABOUT BACKPACKS

Backpacks have become very popular, and not only with students. Some of them are made especially for storage in airline overhead compartments. Many of them are made in stylish luggage materials and colors. They distribute the weight evenly across your shoulders and can be very convenient where extensive walking is a part of your trip. Pack them with the heaviest objects close to the back and nearer to the top of the backpack.

Remember that important documents or money should not be kept in a backpack because it is especially vulnerable to pickpockets.

PACKING CHECKLIST

Most seasoned travelers make a checklist to help them remember the essential items they'll need to take with them. It's very frustrating to arrive at your destination and realize you've forgotten something. The cost of replacing it can cut into your travel budget. Here is a suggested list of things that relate to your preparedness and health.

- ☐ Identification of some type, such as a driver license (mandatory if you plan to drive on your trip)
- ☐ Eyeglasses or contact lenses, and lens cleaner
- ☐ Medical papers such as insurance cards and forms, medical alert cards, and extra copy of medical and eyeglass prescriptions
- ☐ Travel papers, which might include an itinerary, tickets, reservation confirmations and receipts, vouchers, directions, packing lists, traveler's checks, and a list of check serial numbers
- ☐ Phone numbers for health care contacts, insurance company, friends and family, bank, and credit cards, as well as account and policy numbers

For Trips Abroad
- ☐ Passports, visas; also take along an extra passport photo and keep it in a safe place separate from your passport
- ☐ A money belt or necklace-style billfold to carry money, credit cards, passport and visa
- ☐ Vaccination/innoculation certificates
- ☐ Addresses and telephone numbers of embassies, consulates, your physician, and people important to you
- ☐ International driver license
- ☐ Translated medical alert and medical insurance cards

18

It is a good idea to clean out your billfold and remove things that proclaim your financial situation, such as country club membership cards. If you are required to carry military ID, keep it well hidden.

Use common sense when packing your carry-on bag. It may be opened by airport security people, so anything of value should not be placed loosely and temptingly on top.

Toiletries

☐ Breath freshener or mouthwash

☐ Feminine hygiene items

☐ Hand soap, dish soap (to wash baby bottles, etc.)

☐ Medications

☐ Nail care equipment, tweezers, scissors

☐ Skin care lotions, sunscreen, lip balm

☐ Tissues, towelettes, cotton balls, swabs

☐ Toothbrushes, toothpaste, dental floss

Miscellaneous Items

☐ First aid kit

☐ Flashlight and extra batteries

☐ *Healthful Travel*

☐ Pocketknife

☐ Sewing kit (needles, thread, scissors, safety pins)

☐ Travel alarm clock

☐ Umbrella and rain gear

A NOTE ABOUT CLOTHING

Because the clothes you take with you depend so much on what kind of a trip you are taking and where you are going, they would be impossible to list here. However, less is best. Most inexperienced travelers have a tendency to overpack and end up wearing only a few outfits.

The most important thing to remember is BE COMFORT-ABLE—and comfortable shoes should be at the top of the list. Also, it is always a good idea, when planning a trip to tropical climates, to take at least one article of warm clothing for unexpected weather changes. For the most part, all articles of clothing should be wash-and-wear for easy maintenance. *Always pack extra underwear and nightclothes in your carry-on luggage in the event your luggage is mis-routed.*

Packing Tips to Remember

❖ Always pack several days ahead of your trip; you can use the checklist in this chapter.

❖ Plan ahead. Determine the proper clothing by checking the general weather conditions and predictions of your destination.

❖ Pack only what you can carry yourself. This is easier with two smaller suitcases. Take an extra fold-up bag to carry your vacation purchases.

❖ Both men and women should coordinate a wardrobe around specific colors and color coordinates.

❖ It is important take a carry-on bag with important prescription medications, overnight items, and travel-size toiletries when flying.

❖ Clothes wrapped in plastic or in plastic bags or tissue paper travel with less wrinkles.

❖ When you travel light, remember that you should be willing to hand-wash essentials.

YOUR MEDICAL KIT and HEALTH TIPS

Although you may not need all the items listed here on your trip, here is a suggested check list for most travelers' needs. Of course, if you are going to remote areas, additional medical kit items will be required. *Be sure all medicines are well labeled and in original containers.* Also check with your physician on all required medications.

☐ Ace bandage

☐ Antiacids

☐ Antibacterial ointment, such as Neosporin or Bacitracin (sold over the counter), or Bactroban (by prescription only)

☐ Antibacterial soap

☐ Anticonstipation medicines (Senakot or Metamusil)

☐ Antidiarrheal medications, such as Immodium or Pepto Bismol (sold over the counter in most states)

☐ Bandage and bandaids

☐ Bandanna

☐ Chapstick

☐ Dark glasses, plus strap (Blue Blockers suggested)

☐ Dental floss, oil of cloves

☐ Diaper rash medication

☐ Disposable wipes

☐ Disposable syringes/needles, if required (obtain from physician authorizing use)

☐ Extra pair of glasses/contact lenses, sunglasses and repair kit (also good to take a copy of your lens prescription)

☐ First aid kit (It's a good idea to take a class in first aid methods, especially if going to remote areas.)

☐ Foot powder (antifungal)

☐ Hearing aid batteries

☐ Insect repellent (use with care when applying on children) DEET is most effective and long acting

☐ Lip balm

☐ Medications, such as aspirin, acetaminophen (Tylenol), and ibuprofen (Advil), anti-motion sickness medications, antihistamines, ear drops and eye ointment, hydrocortisone ear drops and eye ointment (check with your physician)

☐ Moleskin (for prevention of blisters)

☐ Needle and tweezers (for removing splinters)

☐ Oral rehydration packets

☐ Plastic bags

☐ Skin medicines, such as moisturizing creams to relieve sunburn

☐ Sunscreen (at least 30 SPF)

☐ Thermometer

☐ Vitamins

Carry extra medicines with you, and always take a generic prescription written by a physician for such things as blood pressure medicines, heart medicines, insulin, and medicines for chronic illnesses. Talk with your physician about taking a special kit if you are allergic to insect stings (Ana-Kit or Epi-Pen).

MEDICAL INFORMATION SHEET

Travelers with a chronic medical condition should prepare a medical information sheet before the trip and keep it with passport, tickets, and international identification. Ask your physician about pertinent information. Here is what the sheet should contain:

1. Name, Address, and Social Security Number

2. Insurance company name, address, name of policyholder, policy number, Medicare/Medicaid number

3. Address and telephone of a person to notify in case of an emergency and of employer, if appropriate

4. Blood type, if known

5. Brief outline of medical disorders and any abnormal test results, include current medications and dosages (again, use generic names), drug allergies, reasons for hospitalizations, immunizations and dates received

Wear Medi-Alert bracelets if necessary.

IMPORTANT MEDICAL AND HEALTH TIPS

❖ Do not take medications unfamiliar to you. Sometimes side effects are worse than the symptoms for which the medication was intended.

❖ Use care when you put your medications in your hotel room, or stateroom if on a cruise ship. It is not uncommon to hear stories about medications being thrown out or stolen when the rooms are cleaned.

❖ Don't forget that hypodermic needles can be an environmental hazard and it is important to dispose of them properly. It is also very important that you obtain a letter from your doctor giving you permission to carry needles.

❖ Before taking your pills, wash your hands carefully, because it is commonly known that viral infections are transmitted from hand to mouth.

PREVENTING DENTAL PROBLEMS

The key to good dental care is routine dental check-ups and good hygiene. However, it is a good idea to check with your dentist or periodontist prior to making lengthy travel plans just in case you need major repairs. Most dentists recommend that you do not fly for at least three days after significant dental procedures.

Protect Your Teeth While Traveling

❖ Always use bottled water when brushing your teeth to prevent exposure to contaminated water. Don't forget your dental floss. Keep your toothbrush in a clear, dry, protected container. Even placing your toothbrush on a contaminated counter could transmit disease.

❖ If you fear dental discomfort or pain, be prepared and carry medicines which are familiar to you and which your dentist recommends. Acetaminophen (Tylenol) and ibuprofen (Advil), as well as oil of cloves, are favorites for pain relief. Some people like to use a cough medicine containing codeine. Check with your dentist and be sure that you are familiar with the medicines you might use.

An excellent emergency dental kit can be purchased. It is especially useful if you are going to remote regions. To order, call or write, **Campmor, Wenko Parkway 28 Parkway, Upper Saddle River, NJ 07458, #83131-K, $11.99, plus shipping and postage (800) 526-4784.**

KEEPING FIT ENROUTE

EXERCISE ROUTINE WHILE TRAVELING

W ell ahead of the trip, develop an exercise program that can be maintained while you're out of town. Regular jogging is appropriate for some, while others find that a daily walk is best. The important elements of the exercise are that you do it regularly (preferably every day), that you enjoy it, and that it not be too strenuous.

Excessive or extremely vigorous exercise, such as scrambling over archeological ruins or mountain climbing, should be carried out only by those in the best physical condition.

Before attempting any exercises, check with your physician.

Listed below are some suggested exercises you can do while seated in a car, a train or plane for long periods of time. They are designed to release tension and promote circulation. Remember to exhale while you are contracting your muscles and inhale while relaxing.

These exercises should be done in sets of three to five approximately every one to two hours, especially when flying.

❖ Start by tucking your chin to your chest, raise left shoulder toward your left ear and circle your shoulder three times, next do the same with your right shoulder, circling three times when raised to your right ear. Continue this exercise by alternating the shoulders.

❖ Raise your shoulders up for 10 seconds while deeply inhaling, then drop your shoulders and exhale.

❖ Roll your shoulders up close to your ears, then back, down and forward. Try to move in continuous circles.

❖ Grab opposite shoulder with fingers behind and your arm

raised so that your nose is inside your elbow. Pull gently toward the opposite shoulder. Hold for 10 seconds, then alternate with the other side.

❖ With your forearms crossed and hands holding on to your elbows, twist your torso gently to the right hold for 10 seconds, then twist to the left and hold for 10 seconds.

❖ Squeeze your fingers into a fist for 10 seconds and then release for 10 seconds.

❖ Press abdominal muscles into your spine for 10 seconds while inhaling, then relax and exhale.

❖ Pull right knee to your chin for 10 seconds, then relax. Repeat with left knee.

❖ Tense quadriceps (upper thighs) as tight as you can while pressing your feet flat on the floor.

❖ With your legs straight out, pull your toes up and hold for 10 seconds.

❖ With your legs straight, circle your feet three times in one direction and three times in the other direction.

❖ If you are flying, walk around the cabin every hour to give your lower extremities better circulation to minimize swelling of the ankles and feet.

PERSONAL NOTES AND REMINDERS

WHEN YOU REACH
YOUR DESTINATION

HOTEL SAFETY and COMFORT

Most hotels are now required to have smoke and fire alarms, and posted evacuation routes. Familiarize yourself with these fire safety regulations to be prepared in case of emergencies.

1. When you enter a hotel, resort, or even a dude ranch, ask about evacuation plans. Involve your children in information and practices regarding fire safety and what to do in an earthquake.

2. Ask what the fire alarm sounds like so you'll recognize it if it goes off.

3. When you arrive at your room, look for the evacuation instructions nearby, and locate the two nearest exits.

4. Know how to get to the exit when you leave your room.

5. Count the number of doors required to get to the exits, because in a smoke-filled area you could be unable to see.

6. Check to see if the windows in your room can be opened.

7. Many people try to get a room on a lower floor for easy escape, especially if they are handicapped and would have a problem getting out.

8. Keep your room key within easy reach.

9. Always carry a small flashlight and a small emergency kit.

10. High-heeled shoes may prevent your moving fast, so take along slippers or flat shoes that will protect your feet from heat or shattered glass.

11. If you're traveling to remote areas where there are no

smoke alarms or fire detectors, you may find peace of mind in taking along your own smoke alarm.

12. Never smoke in bed.

13. Extinguish cigarettes with water before placing them in a wastebasket.

14. If you suspect a fire, inform the hotel staff and nearby guests if you think the fire alarm must be activated.

15. Notify rescuers of where you are by hanging a large towel or a sheet outside your window.

Remember: *If you use common sense, stay calm, and don't panic, you will have a better chance of surviving in many circumstances, such as earthquake, fire, flood, or personal emergency.*

PERSONAL AWARENESS

It's not unusual while traveling to take some risks, such as night-time sightseeing in unfamiliar places. Here are some tips to increase your level of awareness, and therefore increase your safety.

1. Women should carry purses with a substantial shoulder strap and wear the purse across the body rather than hanging from the shoulder. *Purses with hanging straps can cause falls, especially when going up or down stairs.*

2. Keep your money in a money belt that you can hide around your waist under clothing, or shoulder holster wallets, or in buttoned inside-jacket or trouser pockets. These are good ways to thwart pickpockets.

3. Avoid wearing or carrying expensive jewelry, clothing, or luggage. Even attractive costume jewelry can be a temptation to thieves. If you must wear jewelry or expensive clothing, cover it with a coat or shawl.

4. Reserve ahead for special security or safety needs. Remember, you can't always rely on hotel safes to protect your valuables.

5. If the hotel does not have a SECURITY safe you can trust for your valuables, keep your money belt and valuables with you at all times, even while showering.

6. When traveling alone, avoid visiting sites by yourself—a group provides added protection.

7. If you must carry your passport with you, place it in a buttoned-inside pocket or money belt.

8. Be aware of sudden distractions or ruses. These are designed to take your attention away from personal safety

and are the stock-in-trade of street criminals. One such ruse is having beverages spilled on you in an airport terminal; while one person is wiping the liquid off you, the other is stealing your wallet.

Children, especially in large cities, are known to hold a paper up in front of your face to distract you. As you struggle to fend them off, your pockets are being picked by the child's partner.

9. Always let someone know where you're going and when you will return.

10. If you go shopping, don't load yourself down with packages. These can easily be taken from you.

11. Before you leave, make a list of all your credit card numbers and leave it with someone who can cancel them at your request should they become lost or stolen. Many people subscribe to a credit card service. Carry as few credit cards as possible.

12. Use only labeled taxis, even if someone offers a "deal."

12. Rely on the hotel concierge to arrange for theater tickets, cabs, tours, restaurant reservations, and so on.

13. Carry your own luggage if possible, especially if they contain important documents. Take your purse or wallet with you at all times.

14. Carry a whistle to attract attention. Also available are travel alarms that shriek if activated.

15. Obtain a readable street map of every city you plan to visit. Memorize map routes so you don't have to study them while you walk.

SUGGESTIONS FOR DRIVING SAFELY

Motor vehicle accidents are more common when people are in

unfamiliar areas, fatigued, recovering from jet lag, or after drinking alcohol. When driving, here are some basic rules to remember:

❖ Acquaint yourself with the driving rules of the area, such as driving on the opposite side of the road.

❖ Don't drive immediately after long flights.

❖ It is safer to rent a larger car or van than a smaller compact.

❖ Wear seat belts.

❖ Ice and snow, as well as sand storms, fog, and grazing animals, make unfamiliar roads especially dangerous.

❖ Even if it is not the law, be sure to wear a helmet when driving or riding off-road vehicles or bicycles.

❖ Be sure your car is protected with an anti-theft device. Do not leave valuable objects visible inside the car; use the trunk.

❖ Get good directions before you start out on a drive to avoid getting lost or stranded.

❖ Familiarize yourself with the car's controls and gasoline access.

COMMON ILLNESSES, INJURIES, AND ACCIDENTS

COMMON ILLNESSES, INJURIES, and ACCIDENTS

How to Prevent or Handle Them

The advice given here is meant to help you handle or, more importantly, avoid some of the most common barriers to healthful travel. Additional, more detailed and extensive books on travel medicine are reviewed in the Appendix. No attempt is made to cover everything here.

GASTROINTESTINAL PROBLEMS

Constipation. This problem is not uncommon on trips involving diet changes and hurried schedules. The key to combating it is to drink plenty of liquids and eat foods high in fiber, such as figs, prunes, and dry bran cereal. It may also be helpful to take along some medication with which you are familiar, such as milk of magnesia or other over-the-counter medications or a laxative such as Senokot.

Diarrhea. This may occur approximately 3-5 days into the trip. Many of us call it "the green apple two-step" or "Montezuma's revenge." It is important to replenish lost fluids and electrolytes with a fluid such as Pedialyte (especially for children) also Gatorade is effective and a favorite fluid replenisher of many. An antimotility drug, Immodium, is sold over the counter in most states and comes in a liquid form for children. Always check with your physician.

After being ill, it is essential to start taking fluids slowly in small amounts over the next few hours to prevent dehydration. Avoid drinking alcohol or eating fried, fatty, or spicy foods until you're back to normal. Of course, if you don't improve, see a physician.

Prevention is the best way to avoid diarrhea. Here are some tips:

- Assume that all water is contaminated, even ice cubes.
- Eat only well-cooked meats.
- Eat raw fruits only if you peel them yourself.
- Avoid raw vegetables, including the lettuce in a sandwich.
- Avoid creamy desserts and rich sauces. They are perfect media for bacterial contaminants.

UPPER-RESPIRATORY INFECTIONS

Upper-respiratory infections are common during travel, caused mostly by crowded conditions on airplanes. People are hurried prior to a trip and may have lowered resistance because of lack of sleep. A nasal spray such as Afrin or a decongestant, particularly one like Benadryl, which is safe for children as well as adults, might help to alleviate congestion. Try all medications prior to leaving on your trip so you know whether it makes you sleepy or excited. Find out what works for you best. If you're going to be driving, obviously you'll want to avoid medications that cause sleepiness.

When traveling with children who are sick with recurrent upper-respiratory problems and who have a history of ear infections, you might have a happier trip if you postpone leaving until your child is well. If your sick child can breathe through the nose with minimal congestion, chances are better for a pain-free flight. Make sure you see your physician about any acute or chronic illness before leaving.

EYE PROBLEMS AND IRRITANTS

Sunglasses can protect you from many irritants. If you wear prescription glasses, carry an extra pair. Clip-ons are quite useful, and blue blockers are a must. Decongestant eye drops are available

37

for itchy eyes caused by dust and allergy-causing factors; ask your physician about these. While flying, eye fluid evaporation can cause "dry eye syndrome," which can be avoided if you use an artificial tear solution commonly available over the counter.

Safety glasses are recommended for sports and other strenuous activities. Swimming goggles that fit well will keep out water, chlorine, and other pollutants.

Contact Lenses

If you wear hard contact lenses, beware of the dangers of wearing them too long—tiny blisters can form on the surface of the eye, which can be painful. Take along extra cleaning and wetting solutions. *Never use saliva as a wetting solution because bacteria can injure your cornea.* Your physician may prescribe an ophthalmic antibacterial ointment for you, especially if you're going into the wilderness with little access to medical facilities.

Following is some general advice for contact lens wearers:

1. If you have been wearing contact lenses for only a short time, don't wear them on long trips.

2. Don't wear lenses on long flights at all, especially if you want to sleep.

3. Carry ample wetting agents and apply them frequently while in flight, in air-conditioned areas, in hot and/or dry climates, and in other low-humidity conditions.

4. It is inadvisable to wear contacts while swimming. Never wear them in hot tubs because of bacteria that may cause serious eye infections.

5. Use only bottled water as a wetting agent and for cleaning.

6. Wash hands thoroughly with soap and water before handling contact lenses to avoid contamination with bacteria and foreign substances.

DENTAL PROBLEMS

Be sure to take flossing material and extra toothbrushes. A dental checkup may save you a toothache abroad or avoid other dental problems. (See also "Preventing Dental Problems" on pages 23-24.)

If you experience a loose filling, cap, or crown, you can protect the area from some pain by covering it with wax or gum.

Be cautious when going to an unknown dentist in foreign countries. Fewer dentists are available abroad, and you don't want to have a tooth pulled unless absolutely necessary, which, in some countries may be the custom. If you must see a dentist, make very sure the office looks clean and instruments are properly sterilized.

INJURIES AND ACCIDENTS

Accidents and injuries are the most common reasons people seek care at emergency rooms and hospitals, or medical departments on cruise ships. Some of the most common injuries while traveling are ankle sprains, knee injuries, and fractures of the arm or wrist. A few pointers might save you from these injuries:

❖ Take care when walking, especially on uneven surfaces, such as cobblestone, streets or walkways with potholes, and when stepping off curbs.

❖ Be sure the soles of your shoes are not slippery. Some shoes could be dangerous on smooth walking surfaces and wet streets.

❖ Slips and falls commonly occur in bathrooms when there is water around the tub or shower. Watch your step on those beautiful marble hotel lobby floors too.

❖ Hold on to a railing while going up or down stairways, escalators, aboard cruise ships, and on other potentially dangerous walkways.

❖ Acquaint yourself with your surroundings. Accidents can

happen anywhere. Be alert to the placement of objects like suitcases stored in an inappropriate location.

❖ When walking at night, always use a flashlight if the lighting is inadequate.

❖ Don't forget that faucets in foreign countries may be marked differently. "C" may mean hot (or *caliente* in Spanish), not cold. In French, "C" means *chaud*, or hot. Burns can occur with poor plumbing facilities, so test the water first to prevent scalding.

❖ Wash scratches and cuts well with soap and water several times a day to keep them from getting infected. Also, take along an antibacterial ointment such as Neosporin. A very effective new ointment, called Bactroban, is also available by prescription.

FOOT PROBLEMS

Before you leave, break in your shoes so they are comfortable. Wool socks, available for extended wear while hiking and camping, are excellent. Use moleskin on your feet at the first sign of pressure to avoid blisters. If you have foot problems, see a podiatrist before your trip so your feet will be in good condition.

BACK PROBLEMS

Many travelers have back problems and others are vulnerable to back pains and strains. The best way to avoid these problems is to prevent them. If you don't sleep well on a soft bed, ask the hotel prior to arrival if firmer mattresses are available, or if a backboard can be inserted between the mattress and box spring. Take aspirin or another pain remedy at the first sign of pain. Seek immediate medical help for pain that radiates into your legs or when they tingle or feel numb or weak.

Tips to Help You Avoid Back Pain

❖ When sitting in airline seats, place a pillow in the small of your back. On long flights, get up and walk around every 30 or 45 minutes.

❖ If you are short and your feet don't reach the floor when sitting in an airplane or other seat, put something on the floor to use as a footrest. If you are tall, try to get a bulkhead or an aisle seat so that you can stretch your legs and no one in front of you will be leaning back on your legs.

❖ When riding in a vehicle for long periods, place a cushion (preferably one that is porous and that allows air to circulate through it) in your lower back area.

❖ While driving, keep the seat in a position so that your knees are approximately at a 30-degree angle above your hips when your feet are touching the control pedals. Also, stop, get out, walk around, and stretch approximately every hour to avoid back stress and pain.

❖ Avoid extra soft chairs, couches, particularly in hotel lobbies and rooms. Soft furniture places abnormal strains on your back.

❖ Kneeling on a chair prevents undue stress on the lower back when bending over bathroom sinks to shave, apply makeup, or wash your hair.

❖ To lift heavy objects, stand close to them, squat down, keep your back straight, and let your legs do the lifting.

People often forget that back problems are directly related to their feet and footwear. For example, on a skiing trip you may be spending considerable time in ski boots. This is not the customary footwear for most people, and you can create problems if you walk around in ski boots for extended periods. Women should wear shoes with heels that are approximately 1½" or lower, and should avoid changing from high heels to low or flat heels frequently.

If you're going on a sporting vacation, the best advice is to take lessons from a professional, no matter what the sport. Even if you have gone skiing or snorkeling before, if it has been a long time since the last outing, a refresher lesson is probably wise.

A vacation is not the time to begin physical exercise regimens. Get in shape well before you leave with exercises that are designed particularly for your sport. Remember that brisk, continuous walking is the best exercise of all, and swimming is also an excellent all-around workout. Continue any regular exercise program that you have become accustomed to, if possible.

If back pain occurs, some old-fashioned cures may be helpful—firm mattresses, bed boards, sleeping on the floor, or on a mattress on the floor. Hot baths or showers can relieve spasms and pain. Ice applications also relieve pain. Pharmacies and travel stores carry heating pads and ice bags that are portable and chemically activated by adding water.

Bed rest is the best treatment for backache but is rarely possible while traveling. Therefore, rest as much as you can under the circumstances and lie on your side in the fetal position, first on the left and then on the right (or vice versa), or on your back with a support under your knees. Do not lie on your stomach.

ALLERGIES

Your routine allergy medications should be kept in well-labeled bottles and in sufficient additional quantities, especially if you are known to have problems with sneezing, itchy eyes, or other reactions to flora and fauna. Tell your physician where you are going and if you have allergies to specific foods or bee stings.

SLEEPLESSNESS

Keep in mind that unfamiliar surroundings may cause sleep problems. Some people take along ear plugs and eye masks to help them achieve a better rest. Sometimes a walk on the beach or in the mountains, or a glass of warm milk or a light liquor refreshment, is helpful. If you are taking medications, be careful when celebrating with cocktails!

MOTION SICKNESS

Motion sickness usually affects children more than adults. Symptoms combine dizziness and nausea. If traveling by car, make sure the car seats are high enough that the child can look at the horizon. Some medications are helpful, such as Bonine and Dramamine; discuss them with your physician. For those over 12 years of age, the patch behind the ear, called Transderm Scope, can last up to 12 hours. However, the patch does cause some side effects, such as dry mouth and drowsiness. Also it's important to eat lightly and to avoid heavy foods.

SKIN RASHES AND SUNBURN

Transient skin rashes may appear when you're traveling. Dry skin can cause itching, especially in warmer areas of the body, such as armpits. Take along a lubricating cream and sunscreen. Hydrocortisone might help to soothe contact dermatitis rashes.

Insect protection may be important where you're going; a spray called DEET is an effective deterrent on skin. Remember that perfumes attract insects, so consider foregoing them. Always wear shoes. Talk to your physician about your planned destination. *Be careful when using insect repellents on children.* Permethrin aerosol can be sprayed on clothing and is very effective for repelling insects off children.

Sunscreens protect you from ultraviolet A and B light, which can be damaging to the skin and may even lead to skin cancer. Apply sunscreens with at least 30 SPF (Sun Protection Factor) and consider wearing reflective cover-up clothing.

There are many reasons for skin rashes while traveling. Ask yourself these questions:

1. When and where did my rash start?

2. Does it itch?

3. Does it seem to be associated with a particular travel

43

activity, medication I am taking (orally or locally on the skin), chemical, perfume, cream, or being close to poison ivy or another plant that may cause a rash?

4. Do I notice any other symptoms associated with the rash?

Keeping skin moisturized is the key ingredient to preventing itching. Even the most robust traveler should be concerned about flaky, itchy, dry, and cracking skin. Frequent swimming, scuba diving, and sun contact may dry skin even more. The following points might be helpful:

❖ Water-based sunscreens lubricate the skin better than oily ones. Apply when skin is moist, such as after a bath or shower.

❖ Among the soaps that are kind to the skin are Dove, Basis, and Lubriderm.

❖ In the tropics, shower immediately after swimming to prevent the many different organisms and irritants from causing a variety of rashes.

❖ Be sure that when using spas they are properly sanitized and check on what chemicals are used in the water.

JET LAG

Everyone knows that crossing time zones quickly upsets our circadian rhythm, or 24-hour clock. All of our bodily functions—digestive, mental, psychological, sleep—are disturbed. For some travelers, this could mean that they are having important business meetings at three o'clock in the morning, or they're "out on the town" at eleven o'clock in the morning or having "breakfast" meetings at ten o'clock at night—all on their "home" time.

The poor concentration, shortened attention span, and intestinal problems resulting from disturbing the circadian rhythm, known as jet lag, is not only bad for business but can ruin any trip.

One of the keys to overcoming jet lag is a positive, good-natured attitude, especially at the start of a trip. If you are a rigid, critical person, try to become aware of this and lighten your attitude.

Are you an early riser or do you need to sleep in? "Nightingales," or late risers—people who work or play late into the evening—have more trouble traveling east and less trouble traveling west. "Larks," people who retire early and rise early, have the reverse condition, and do better traveling from west to east.

❖ Prepare for the battle against jet lag by determining the time difference between your home and your destination and start eating and sleeping according to your destination's schedule. This may be difficult to do, and if you can't begin your time adaptation in advance, simply increasing your awareness may help condition your attitude before you leave.

❖ If possible, schedule your arrival so that you have the time to adjust to the time difference.

❖ While on route to your destination, set your watch to the destination time. This will help you adjust your eating and sleeping habits.

❖ Minimize the consumption of alcohol, and stay away from tobacco smoke completely, as these factors compound jet lag problems.

❖ If you must arrive in the morning, a very short nap is advisable on arrival, followed by a shower to increase your alertness.

❖ Initially at least, stay away from intensely mental activities such as crucial negotiations, gambling, or important decision making. Delay these until after you've adjusted somewhat.

❖ To induce sleep in your new time zone, try to sleep at the same time each night. Long hot showers and mild exercise are suggested, but avoid strenuous exercise before you go

45

to sleep. Remember, brisk walking is the best exercise. (Over-the-counter products or other commercial inducements to sleep are not recommended.)

❖ A snack high in carbohydrates before bedtime will increase drowsiness. Avoid stimulants such as tea, coffee, hot chocolate, soft drinks, and alcohol prior to bedtime.

❖ Get up reasonably early every morning regardless of how much sleep you have had, and eat protein-rich meals about the same time each day. This will get your circadian rhythm adjusted.

❖ Sitting by the window of the airplane and taking in the sunlight may help you adjust as you are arriving at your destination. Recent research indicates that our 24-hour clock is governed by light from the sun, which we perceive through sight. This controls the production of hormones, including melatonin, which control our day and night cycles.

Jet lag *will* go away, and the speed of its departure depends on how you handle the following things:

1. Adjust as much as possible to the destination time before you leave.

2. Exercise while traveling and with brisk walking or other mild exercise after arrival.

3. Avoiding drinking alcohol and being around tobacco smoke while traveling.

4. Keep regular sleeping and eating hours when you arrive.

5. Take a short nap when you arrive if possible.

6. Avoid too much activity until after you have adjusted.

OVERHEATING

It is important in hot climates—especially in the tropics—to stay in air-conditioned hotels if possible. Wear as much heat-reflecting clothing as possible, drink extra fluids, and decrease your alcohol intake. Avoid outdoor activities from 10:00 a.m. to 2:00 p.m., the longest sun exposure period.

❖ Salt tablets are not necessary in hot climates as long as you eat a normal diet containing a proper amount of salt and if you eat plenty of fresh fruits and vegetables that have been washed in safe water.

❖ In areas where you can't trust the drinking water, use bottled water and soft drinks to be safe.

❖ Recognizing the early signs of overheating will help serious heat problems. If headaches, dizziness, muscle cramps and general sluggishness occur, get out of the sun immediately, drink fluids, bathe, or find cooler surroundings such as an air-conditioned room, even in an automobile when available. If nothing else, find shade, lie down, and rest.

❖ The evaporation of perspiration helps to cool us. Heat problems are aggravated in hot, humid areas because the cooling effects of evaporation are inhibited by moist air. Desert areas can be much more easily tolerated as long as you drink plenty of fluids.

❖ In hot climates, wear loose cotton clothing and a broad-brimmed hat. The area around the head should be protected by an air space above the crown area with ventilation holes for air circulation. Baseball caps offer little protection.

HIGH-ALTITUDE PROBLEMS

If you plan to travel to areas that are 8,000 feet (2,600 meters) or higher, you should be prepared for the effects of high altitude even if you are young and physically fit.

❖ If you travel quickly to your destination by airplane, give

47

yourself a day or two to acclimate yourself before engaging in strenuous exercise.

❖ It is best to travel to higher altitudes gradually, approximately 2,000 feet per day, in order to allow your body to adjust to the change in oxygen levels and atmospheric pressure.

❖ Do not sleep at the maximum altitude reached each day, but descend to a lower altitude.

❖ As is true under any circumstances of exertion, drink plenty of fluids to compensate not only for the normal fluid loss and more rapid breathing, but also for the dryness of high altitudes.

❖ Avoid smoking tobacco under any circumstances, and don't drink alcoholic beverages. Take no chances whatsoever without expert advice concerning the effects of medications at high altitudes—consult a physician.

❖ If you experience headaches, inability to sleep, dizziness, depression, or anxiety, you may be suffering from acute mountain sickness.

❖ Keep in mind that oxygen is not a cure for altitude sickness. Although there are prescription drugs that can be taken to alleviate symptoms, aspirin or buffered aspirin is usually helpful in alleviating most of them.

❖ If you experience discomfort, descending rapidly (approximately 1,000 feet) will usually relieve your symptoms. If that cannot be done, take in oxygen until you can descend.

Acute mountain sickness can be compounded by hypothermia. This is caused by the loss of body heat faster than it is produced, resulting in the inability to maintain a core temperature of 98.6. Such loss is aggravated by wind and wet clothing or immersion in cold water. For example, excessive perspiration inside wind- and rain-proof clothing can cause your clothing to become completely drenched. Get dry and warm immediately to prevent hypothermia.

WHAT TO DO IF SEVERELY ILL OVERSEAS

If you become sick overseas or are badly injured in an accident, the following pointers might be helpful:

❖ If there is time, telephone your own physician for advice. (That's why you carry your physician's name and phone number with you.) Before you leave, find out what kind of night and weekend availability your physician provides.

❖ When telephoning provide a quick update on your medical background to refresh your physician's memory in case your file is not available for reference. (See the list in the Your Medical Kit and Health Tips chapter, page 21.)

❖ Included in the Appendix are a few foreign medical terms that can aid you in getting immediate help for illness or injury if you don't speak the language or don't have an interpreter at hand. (See page 118)

❖ Remember, the quickest way to a hospital emergency room is usually by taxi. Many hotels, in an emergency, will help you by supplying a car from the hotel. Don't be shy in asking for help.

❖ If your problem is not immediately life-threatening, you may wish to fly home so your personal physician can solve the problem. Special travel insurance and evacuation services are listed in the Appendix.

If you are treated abroad, it is essential that you bring home documents of your evaluation and treatment.

There is a list of recommended reading in the Appendix for books covering, more in depth, medical problems while traveling .

49

PERSONAL NOTES AND REMINDERS

SUGGESTIONS FOR SPECIFIC TRAVELERS

CRUISE TRAVELING

Taking a cruise can be one of the most relaxing kinds of vacations. You are completely catered to, and you can participate in all the planned activities or just lie on deck and read. While taking a cruise there are things to be aware of for a more enjoyable time.

❖ Notify cruise line ahead of time to inform them of any special problems you have.

❖ Protect yourself from the sun: liberally apply sunscreen, wear sunglasses, and use a wide-brimmed hat.

❖ Watch your step going from deck to deck—hang onto the railings.

❖ When participating in the varied sports activities, warm up first and don't overdo.

❖ When visiting ports, watch what you eat and drink.

❖ Review the pertinent safety tips in "Your Medical Kit and Health Tips." A common reason for visiting the pharmacy or cruise doctor is for medical items left at home. Use the checklist starting on page 21.

Seasickness—Don't Let it Spoil Your Trip

❖ Take Dramamine or another motion-sickness preventer one hour before the ship sets sail. (Pregnant women can take ginger root capsules—two every four to six hours.)

❖ Eat lightly, but don't let the stomach get empty.

❖ Remember when booking your cabin, you will experience the least motion on midship and lower decks.

❖ Fresh air helps alleviate motion sickness, small enclosed spaces make it worse. Focus on the horizon.

The FREQUENT BUSINESS TRAVELER

A dvance planning is a must for the executive. The following tips should make your business trip more pleasant:

❖ Stay in a top-of-the-line hotel if you are alone. It's usually safer, more impressive to prospective clients, and provides more entertainment facilities.

❖ In unfamiliar areas, take cabs for short trips instead of walking.

❖ Don't overlook networking in other cities with organizations of which you are a member. Call ahead to check on meeting schedules, dinners, or special events.

❖ Take only the number of suitcases you can carry yourself.

❖ If giving presentations at meetings, send the information to your hotel before you leave. Travel is less stressful if you don't have to carry all your materials.

❖ Keep track of the best restaurants if you travel to the same city frequently.

❖ If you don't like to dine alone, ask your hotel concierge to obtain a ticket for you to attend a cultural event or other entertainment where lunch or dinner is included.

❖ Remember that your objective is to enjoy yourself, as well as accomplish your business goals.

SPECIAL TIPS FOR THE WOMAN EXECUTIVE

❖ Don't be afraid to ask the hotel concierge or desk clerk to provide an escort to accompany you to your room if someone there makes you feel uncomfortable.

❖ You might find it more relaxing—and safer—to order dinner in your room.

❖ Travel with very little jewelry. Even high-quality costume jewelry may be appealing to thieves.

The WOMAN
TRAVELING SOLO

E ven if you have a mate or a significant other, sometimes the best vacation may be traveling solo, so that each of you can enjoy exploring things that the other person does not find interesting.

Traveling Solo, by Jennifer Cecil, is an excellent and informative book that lists more than 300 locations where you may travel and share communal dining activities. It has a special section on new-age retreats. It is excellent for women who wish to travel alone, and gives information about tours for those from 18 to 38 as well as those over 50.

Cecil, an expert on Caribbean travel, discusses travel in the United States, Canada, Central America, and the Caribbean. Chapters cover a wide range of activities, including "Just Relaxing in Cozy Inns," "Learning a Foreign Language," "Cooking Schools," "Painting, Potting, and Photographing," "Volunteering to Save the Planet," and "Fly Fishing." Each has an extensive bibliography that lists helpful books, information, and newsletters on specific activities or hobbies.

Refer to the Appendix for many helpful listings for solo travelers.

It is important to remember certain rules, especially when traveling alone or with another female.

❖ Stay in better hotels, dress conservatively, and leave your expensive jewelry at home.

❖ Ignore offensive verbal comments and eye contact with aggressive people, and;

❖ Be careful when making "new friends," even on a romantic cruise.

❖ If you have chronic gynecological problems, see your physician before leaving on an extensive trip abroad. Hygiene standards in other areas and other countries may not be what you are accustomed to at home. Be sure you pack extra feminine hygiene supplies.

❖ It is common with travel stresses, commitments, and jet lag for biological functions such as your menstrual period to be irregular or even "shut off," especially when crossing multiple time zones.

❖ A regular exercise program is recommended before, during, and after your trip.

❖ If you are on birth control pills, altitude sickness may be worse. Watch your salt intake because you tend to retain more fluid while on birth control pills. The effectiveness of your birth control pills may be diminished by illness such as vomiting or diarrhea. If either should occur within three hours of taking your birth control pill, take another one or you may not be protected. Also, be aware that condoms and rubber diaphragms can disintegrate in hot weather.

❖ If you have the slightest suspicion you might be pregnant, take a pregnancy test before you leave. The first weeks can be crucial, and strenuous traveling and stress could be dangerous to the fetus.

❖ To prevent yeast infections and uncomfortable rashes, let your body breathe. Wearing tight underwear, shorts, and jeans invites problems. Cotton underwear breathes better. Avoid yeast infections by changing out of wet bathing suits, especially in hot, humid weather.

TRAVELING WITH CHILDREN

I t's surprising to learn how much children remember about vacations and traveling. Just think for a moment about some of the fun you had as a child on trips. You can use travel to expose your children to new experiences and family togetherness and to build memories for tomorrow.

To ensure that everyone will have a good time, decide what type of trip is appropriate for the age of your child or children. Traveling with children is rarely all fun and games. Expect the inevitable squabbles, innumerable bathroom stops, an endless need for drinks and snacks, and a host of minor illnesses and injuries. This chapter is about making travel fun and safe for your child or children and, most of all, *for you.*

GENERAL COMMENTS

Be ready for the unexpected. Children are unpredictable and may become ill, overtired, bored, or just different from the way they are at home. To cut down the stress on both you and your offspring, plan ahead.

Be realistic about vacation expectations. Think about your children's ages and how busy they are at home. Before taking them on long trips, try a few short ones to see how they react. This will help to indicate how well they will travel.

If you wish to take a vacation when your children are young (between the ages of 2 and 7 years), you may want to spend part of your vacation traveling with them and part without them. Children will change the way you travel, and the key to having a good trip is careful planning.

TIPS FOR TRAVELING WITH CHILDREN

1. Bring with you written information from your physician if your child has a chronic illness or allergy, is on medication, or has a significant health condition. Most pediatricians and family physicians can provide safety facts dealing with each age during your child's development.

2. Most cities have children's hospitals with associated urgent care centers nearby—usually the best places for your child to be cared for in case of accident or illness.

3. If you must call your child's physician while traveling, before you leave find out how best to do this, and tell the operator placing your call whether the situation is an emergency or a routine matter.

4. Remember to carry plastic bags, and moist towlettes for accidents.

5. Buy appropriate, well-made car restraint seats, if you are traveling by car. Some families even carry car seats with them to save added cost while traveling abroad.

6. Children should never be left alone in a car for any reason.

7. It is important to expect appropriate conduct in the car when traveling with children. Seat belts are helpful in keeping children restrained and quiet.

8. Temporarily baby-proofing any location you visit is a *must*.

9. Swimming pools are always dangerous. Do not permit children near them without responsible adult supervision.

10. Be extra cautious during picnics and barbecues where children can be easily burned.

11. With plane travel, make sure infants are sucking on a bottle or pacifier during ascent and descent. This helps

their ears pop with changing cabin pressure. Older children may chew gum. Do not let children suck on hard candy or lollipops because these may become lodged in the throat if there is turbulence.

12. If a child has an ear infection, travel is usually safe if the pain has gone and treatment has been started to cure the infection. Generally, if a child can breathe through the nose, air and mountain travel are less likely to cause ear pain that results from pressure changes. Nasal sprays (such as Afrin) and decongestants may be quite helpful. Benadryl is effective because it may make a child sleepy and is sold over the counter in most states. Try medication ahead of time so that you know its effect.

13. Apply sun screen to your children's exposed skin in hot climates, and have them wear sunglasses. Sunscreens with protection no less than 30 SPF are recommended.

14. Make sure your children wear shoes at all times to prevent cuts and abrasions. Shoes are particularly important around water to minimize slips and falls.

15. A child gains a sense of independence by having a personal knapsack, suitcase, or travel bag. It is also good training to help children count the number of things they are carrying so that they can be sure they have all their belongings as you go from place to place. It's usually not possible to return to the location for a lost item while traveling.

16. A favorite blanket, toy, game, coloring book, or picture book may make travel more enjoyable. (Many games and activities are available in your local bookstore.)

17. It is very helpful to take sandwiches, small cans of juice, crackers, and dry cereal on a trip because children always seem to be hungry, especially when there can't be a

structured meal time. For younger infants (if they are on formula), an adapter for your automobile cigarette lighter can be used to warm bottles or soups.

18. Be prepared with additional refills if your child is on medication. Also, if the child is allergic to any medication, make sure a Medi-Alert bracelet is worn.

19. Be prepared with "spare change" (a self-contained change of diapers), plastic bags, medicines (especially items such as Benadryl and Tylenol), whistle, lip balm, insect repellent, and a first aid kit.

20. Safety awareness is essential, especially around the holidays, moving day, or while visiting relatives. Purses belonging to relatives may pose a real danger if they contain medication.

21. Don't leave your child alone with anyone that isn't highly recommended. Make sure babysitters have written instructions, and check their resumes or if they are bonded. At the end of this chapter are helpful instructions for babysitters.

JOINT FAMILY TRAVELING

Here's something to think about when planning a vacation. You and your children could find greater enjoyment by sharing your vacation with another family. A single parent can find this a terrific way to have fun and travel with companions. If you are thinking about this, here are a few pointers.

❖ When planning your trip or vacation, be sure that the joint families have the same expectations. Discuss the details before travel time.

❖ Discuss the handling of finances. Clear any misunderstanding in this area to rule out any resentment during the trip.

❖ Discuss the sharing of duties and which activities you can enjoy together and separately.

❖ Obviously, it is best that you know that the children enjoy each other's company and are close to the same age and that the adults find each other congenial.

❖ Discipline by parents may vary. Be aware of this and respect each other's discipline styles.

CHILDREN AND ILLNESS

A few key points to keep your children healthy while traveling:

❖ It is well known that diseases are carried by hands to the mouth, so it is most important to keep little hands out of mouths as much as possible.

❖ Keep children from putting dirt or sand in their mouths.

❖ Always have them avoid ingesting tap water while brushing teeth or while in the bath or shower.

❖ Check with travel clinics, many of which are associated with children's hospitals, to get updates on required immunizations or malaria prophylaxis, especially if your children are part of a larger number of children traveling with parents in a group.

❖ Remember that children are strongly affected by extreme temperature changes. For instance, prepare for the chilly air conditioning on airplanes by "layer dressing" children well (clothing them in items that can added and removed as necessary). Also, children's skin can burn very quickly, so always apply sunscreen.

❖ Children are irresistibly drawn to touch animals and never think about the consequences of bites or scratches. Keep them away from animals, especially monkeys.

❖ Don't forget to give extra liquids to infants and children to prevent dehydration. Also remember that exotic foods are not well tolerated by children and infants.

❖ If you must use insect repellents on children, do so with caution. Keep their hands away from their eyes and mouth as much as possible. Spray clothing with insecticide containing Pemethin.

❖ Oral rehydrating solutions for dealing with diarrhea are available in dried packets. Common solutions are Pedialyte, and Lytrin. Check with your physician regarding the most current recommendations.

INSTRUCTIONS FOR TRAVELING WITH INFANTS

Traveling with a baby presents a set of needs different from traveling with potty-trained children three years of age or older. For one thing you need extra planning and equipment.

Suggested Baby Equipment

☐ Baby food and plastic spoon, formula, juice

☐ Bathing supplies (towel, washcloth, soap, shampoo, powder, lotions and creams)

☐ Bottle warmer, bottles, nipples, caps, and pacifiers

☐ Car seat (excellent for airlines and rental cars)

☐ Child wrist hand-holder

☐ Diaper bag, disposable diapers, changing pads

☐ Medications, vitamins, thermometer

☐ Nail clippers

☐ Night light

☐ Nursing pads, burp pads, bib

☐ Portable crib or playpen, waterproof crib sheets, blankets

☐ Potty seat

☐ Small plastic bowl with lid & training cup

☐ Umbrella stroller (optional)

☐ Zip-close plastic bags

General Planning

❖ Buy equipment that is good for travel.

❖ Check with your pediatrician.

❖ Bring Tylenol.

❖ Bring a thermometer.

❖ Bring Ipecac (to induce vomiting; use only with physician's instructions).

❖ Bring your pediatrician's phone number.

❖ Provide your child with an identification tag.

❖ Bring along significant medical history, if pertinent.

❖ Set realistic expectations and priorities—consider yourself.

Air Travel

❖ Choose flight time carefully—fly nonstop if possible.

❖ Ask for a seat assignment when making reservations.

❖ Try to obtain an empty seat next to you.

❖ Help your baby adjust to air pressure changes.

Car Travel

❖ Bring liquids, snacks—a day's worth of supplies.

❖ Allow for hot and cold climate needs.

❖ Plan for "stretch" time as necessary.

❖ A car seat is a must.

❖ Think ahead about sleep patterns and schedules.

❖ Bring a variety of toys.

Train Travel

❖ Make reservations well in advance—consider family seating.

❖ Carry your own essentials, such as toilet paper, soap, towels, blankets or coats.

❖ Take along extra snacks.

Destinations

❖ Always make motel reservations—ask for adequate space and privacy.

❖ Consider diaper service or disposable diapers.

❖ Consider renting baby furniture.

Restaurants

❖ Choose restaurants carefully.

❖ Adjust eating times.

❖ Consider drive-throughs and impromptu picnics for added fun.

❖ Bring your child's own utensils.

U.S. CHILDREN'S MUSEUMS

Children's Discovery Museum of San Jose, 180 Woz Way, San Jose, CA 95110-2780, (408) 298-5437

Tech Museums of Innovation, 145 W. San Carlos St., San Jose, CA 95113, (408) 279-7150

Bay Area Discovery Museum, 557 E. Ft. Baker, Sausalito, CA 94965, (415) 332-9646

Children's Museum of Denver, 2121 Crescent Dr., Denver, CO 80211, (303) 433-7444

Chicago Children's Museum, North Pier, 465 E. Illinois, Chicago, IL 60611, (312) 527-1000

Children's Museum of Indianapolis, 3000 N. Meridian St., Indianapolis, IN 46208, (317) 924-5431

Lied Discovery Children's Museum, 833 Las Vegas Blvd. N., Las Vegas, NV 89101, (702) 382-KIDS

Magic House St. Louis Children's Museum, 516 S. Kirkwood Rd., St. Louis, MO 63122, (314) 822-8900

Brooklyn Children's Museum, 145 Brooklyn Ave., Brooklyn, NY 11213, (718) 735-4400

Children's Museum of Memphis, 2525 Central Ave., Memphis, TN 38104, (901) 458-2678

Capitol Children's Museum, 800 Third St., N.E., Washington, DC 20002, (202) 543-8600

BOOKS AND DESTINATION GUIDES

Adventuring with Children: The Complete Manual for Family Adventure Travel by Nan and Kevin Jeffrey (Avalon House, 1991), 330 pages, $14.95

Frommer's has a series of excellent family travel guides including *New York City with Kids, California with Kids, Los Angeles with Kids, San Francisco with Kids,* and *Washington D.C. with Kids,* Prentice Hall, around $18.00 each.

Innocents Abroad: Traveling with Kids in Europe by Valerie Wolf Deutsch and Laura Sutherland (Penguin, 1991), 480 pages, $15.95

Kidding Around London: A Young Person's Guide to the City (John Muir Publications, 1990), 63 pages, $9.95 to $12.95. The *Kidding Around* series gives the same breezy treatment to other cities, including Paris, Washington, San Francisco, Los Angeles, and New York.

Recommended Family Inns of America (Globe Pequot, 1989), 312 pages, $12.95

Take Your Kids to Europe by Cynthia W. Harriman (Mason-Grant Publications, 1991), 222 pages, $12.95

Travel with Children (2nd ed.) by Maureen Wheeler (Lonely Planet Publications, 1990), 160 pages, $10.95

Traveling with Children and Enjoying It: A Complete Guide to Family Travel by Car, Plane, and Train by Arlene Kay Butler (Globe Pequot Press, 1991), 256 pages, $11.95

RESOURCES FOR CHILDREN WITH DISABILITIES

National Parent Network on Disabilities, (703) 684-6763, 1600 Prince, Suite 115, Alexandria, VA 22314. Provides advice ranging from babysitters to special programs. For monthly magazine, *Exceptional Parent*, call (800) E-PARENT. Address is 20 State St., Hackensack, NJ 07601-5421

National Handicapped Sports, 451 Hungerford, Suite 100, Rockville, MA 20850,(301) 217-0960

National Handicapped Sports, Tahoe Handicapped Ski School, 5946 Illinois Ave., Orangevale, CA 95662.

Winter Park Program for the Blind, P.O. Box 36 Winter Park, Co 80482, (303) 726-5514.

BABYSITTER INFORMATION SHEET

This form is borrowed from the California Medical Association.

FACT SHEET FOR THIS DATE ONLY_____

Where we will be _____

Phone _____

Will return by_____

Special instructions: _____

_____

_____

_____

MEALS: Give no food except _____ **at** _____

_____ **at** _____

SLEEP: _____
(when, clothes, blankets, window, heat)

BATH: at _____. **DON'T LEAVE CHILD ALONE!**

PLAY: _____
(Where are toys, books, clothes. Avoid: stove, hot water, stairs, sharp objects, medicine, machines, open windows, electricity, street, animals, matches.)

OTHER INSTRUCTIONS:

1. Keep outside doors locked (from inside only), and don't open for strangers.

2. Keep phone lines open for important calls. I expect the following deliveries and calls—here's what to do:

_____

_____

_____

3. Special (medication needed, flashlight, etc.)

_____

_____

_____

_____

_____

_____

Use back of this sheet for messages or information for us.

SUCCESSFUL FAMILY CAMPING

Spurred by a love of the outdoors, limited funds, or both, carloads of campers head to parks and campgrounds in search of peace, quiet, and economical fun. Most will find camping a relaxing experience, but some will get more than they bargained for because of injuries and accidents. Most accidents can be avoided with a little common sense and preparation.

Camping with children can be a wonderful family experience and it can be an an affordable way to spend great quality time with the kids. Bring along plenty of entertainment, such as storybooks or nature books about the area you're going to visit. Traveling with other families helps to occupy children.

SUGGESTED CAMPING EQUIPMENT

- ☐ Tent, poles, stakes
- ☐ Tarp or groundcover
- ☐ Sleeping bags
- ☐ Air mattresses, cots, foam pads
- ☐ Folding chairs, campstools
- ☐ Folding table
- ☐ Air pump for inflatables
- ☐ Heater, camp fuel, propane canisters
- ☐ Lantern and fuel, flashlights and extra batteries
- ☐ Patch kit for tent, raft, air mattresses, bicycle tires, etc.
- ☐ Saw, hatchet, axe, folding shovel, hammer and nails

- [ ] Rope, string
- [ ] Clothesline and clothespins
- [ ] Whisk broom
- [ ] Portable toilet, toilet paper, plastic bags, chemical deodorant/disinfectant
- [ ] Binoculars, compass, whistle
- [ ] Pocketknife
- [ ] Heavy gloves
- [ ] First aid kit and book, snake bite kit
- [ ] Blankets, pillows
- [ ] Towels, washcloths
- [ ] Matches, lighter
- [ ] Firewood, charcoal, kindling
- [ ] Cooking pans, utensils
- [ ] Paper plates and eating utensils

RULES FOR CAMPING HEALTH AND SAFETY

The Campsite

❖ Choose a campsite carefully to ensure the cooking area is away from brush, overhanging trees, and other fire hazards.

❖ In areas where flash floods may be a hazard, select a campsite on higher ground, especially the sleeping areas.

❖ Arrange tents so that there are obvious pathways or "camp streets" to help people avoid tripping over tent poles and other hazards in the dark.

❖ Check your flashlights and batteries well in advance so that you don't find yourself at a remote location with very little or no light source.

Protection From Burns and Fires

Burns are among the most common and preventable campground injuries, especially among small children. Watch children at all times around campfires, stoves, and lanterns. One person should be in charge of the cooking at any one time. This promotes responsibility and avoids the ambiguity of several people thinking that others are taking care of business.

Camp stoves and heaters are explosive devices if not checked and handled properly. If they are left on during the night while you are sleeping, they can cause carbon monoxide poisoning and explosions. Extinguish all campfire embers, and carefully secure volatile fuel stoves.

On Use of Sharp Implements

Cuts from camping knives and other sharp implements are common. Use the knife or axe before leaving home to get a feel for its sharpness. Also, when chopping wood, wear something to protect your eyes from flying chips. Always wear boots or shoes while chopping wood.

Food Preparation

Food should be properly cooked and handled. Ground or mashed protein dishes tend to spoil quicker than solid ones. For example, ground meats, tuna and egg salads, or any food prepared with dairy products are invaded by bacteria if left to stand for only a short while and should be eaten immediately.

Sliced ham will resist spoiling longer than ground hamburger. Tuna salad should be prepared from the can at the site rather than prepared beforehand and carried with you.

The surfaces where poultry and other raw meats are prepared should be carefully cleaned before and after use to avoid possible salmonella contamination. Cooked meat should not be placed on unclean surfaces.

Clean wild game and fish well, removing intestines and other organs. Thorough washing in safe water is essential. Game should be cooked and eaten promptly to avoid spoilage and contamination.

Transport cold food in coolers, keeping them tightly closed and covered with insulation such as blankets or sleeping bags.

A Word About the Water

Regardless of how safe you may think the water is at a camping location, always boil it before drinking or using it for washing vegetables or brushing your teeth. Boil water from streams, rivers, or lakes for three to five minutes to avoid contamination. Or use a water filter rated to remove *Giardia lamblia*, a parasite that infects the small intestine and can cause severe diarrhea. If possible, take along bottled water. Water purification kits are also available.

Protection from Bites and Allergies

Test insect repellant on a small area of skin prior to the trip to determine if you have any allergic reactions to it. Keep insecticides and repellants away from uncovered food.

If you know that you are allergic to pollen, dust, or other materials likely to be encountered on a camping trip, start taking medication beforehand. Everyone is allergic to poison ivy, poison oak, and sumac, to varying degrees. To avoid exposure, learn to identify these plants, and wear long pants and shoes or boots rather than sandals. Also avoid hanging towels and garments on bushes near streams. Exposure to poisonous plants is particularly prevalent during spring and summer months, when you are more likely to wear shorts and T-shirts.

If you have a chronic medical condition, always locate medical facilities before reserving a campsite. Speak with your physician about the trip in advance.

ADVICE FOR COMMON PROBLEMS

❖ Blisters are a common problem for campers. Don't pop

71

them; instead, cover them with a bandage. The best anti-blister strategy is to wear a good pair of hiking shoes or sneakers. Be sure the shoe has a good arch and a sturdy sole. Pick mid-ankle or high-top styles for stability.

❖ Dehydration is easily avoided. Two to three liters a day of noncaffeinated beverages are recommended. Avoid alcohol.

❖ Altitude sickness is not usually a concern until you reach about 5,000 feet, though this can vary depending on overall health, activity level, and age. Babies and older people often feel the effects of altitude more than others. Headache, blurry vision, and dizziness may occur. Go to a lower altitude to relieve symptoms, but seek medical advice if they persist or are severe.

❖ Campers with asthma tend to have difficulty breathing late at night, when smoke from extinguished campfires settles. Ask your physician in advance whether preventive measures, such as medication changes, make sense for you.

❖ Campers with back problems—and anyone else who does not relish sleeping on hard ground—should take along a good pillow and mattress.

❖ Again, sunscreen is a must. Use one with a sun protection factor of SPF 30 or above because in clean air, campers sunburn more easily than in a smog-blanketed city.

First Aid Kits

Put together an inexpensive first aid kit and carry it with you at all times. Make sure you have these items: a lightweight thermal blanket, a whistle to call for help, a piece of rope about two meters long, bandages, lip balm, sunscreen, a compass, extra socks and shoelaces, waterproof matches and candles, aspirin or acetaminophen, insect repellent, and hydrocortisone cream. Kits are available at camping or sporting goods stores.

RECREATIONAL VEHICLES

Frequently, camping trips involve the use of recreational vehicles. Often these are unfamiliar to you and present additional hazards. Practice driving such vehicles as much as possible before you encounter totally unfamiliar driving situations, such as off-road or wilderness driving.

Carbon monoxide poisoning is always a danger when you have combustion combined with close confinement. Be aware that trucks with camper shells and recreational vehicles with doors or windows located near the exhaust pipe can be very dangerous.

PETS

If at all possible, leave your dogs at home. They can attract ticks, become contaminated with poison oak or poison ivy and then contaminate you. Your pet may encounter wild animals, including skunks, get lost, and fight with dogs belonging to other people. These are situations no one needs on a camping trip.

CAMPING RESOURCES

The Sierra Club, Los Angeles chapter, publishes an activities guide—including camping, hiking, and backpacking information—three times a year. Call (213) 387-4287 or write to Sierra Club, 3345 Wilshire Blvd., Suite 508, Los Angeles, CA 90010.

Go Camping America publishes a free directory of campgrounds and a camping vacation planning guide. Call (800) 47-SUNNY for information.

Camping with Kids by Don Wright (Cottage Press, 1992), 192 pages, $9.95.

Common Sense Outdoor Medicine by Newell D. Breyfogle (Ragged Mountain Press, 1993), 432 pages, $14.95. The book covers a wide variety of subjects that are related to health, including how to predict the weather, nutrition while foraging for food and water and the design of a simple solar still.

Guide to Free USA Campgrounds, (Cottage Press, 1990), 640 pages, $14.95)

Medicine For The Outdoors, A Guide To Emergency Medical Procedures And First Aid by Paul S. Auerbach, M.D. (Little, Brown & Company, 1993), 412 pages, $14.95. An excellent reference work, it covers not only the usual first aid subjects but also disorders related to specific environments such as high altitude, underwater diving, and extreme heat and cold—a must in all outdoor operations requiring a base camp or other central location of operations.

Pocket Guide to Emergency First Aid by the American Medical Association, (Random House, 1993), 86 pages, $3.95. Small enough to carry in your backpack or with your camping equipment, outstanding resource and essential for camping in the wilderness.

Pocket Guide to Wilderness Medicine By Paul G. Gill, Jr., M.D. (Simon & Schuster, 1991), 204 pages, $11.50. For the up-high adventurer, backpacker, and experienced wilderness camper. Pocket-sized but thick, and quite comprehensive, including instructions on building a snow cave or a snow trench for shelter. A particularly valuable section is on eye injuries in the wild. If you're going on a high-risk wilderness outing—don't leave home with out it.

Woodall's Campground Directory, (Wood Publishing, $16.95), a 600-plus-pages, state-by-state listing of more than 15,000 campgrounds and attractions. Regional camping guides are also available for $5.00 from Wood Publishing.

Wilderness with Children by Michael Hodgson (Stackpole Books, 1992, 144 pages, $12.95)

ORGANIZATIONS

American Wilderness Experience, P.O. Box 1486, Boulder, CO 80306, (800) 444-0099

Appalachian Valley Bicycle Touring, 31 East Fort Ave., P.O. Box 27079, Baltimore, MD 21230, (410) 837-8068

Grandtravel, c/o The Ticket Counter, 6900 Wisconsin Ave., #706, Chevy Chase, MD 28015, (800) 247-7651

O.A.R.S. Rafting Adventures, Box 67, Angels Camp, CA 95222, (209) 736-4677

Rascals in Paradise, c/o Adventure Express, 185 Berry St., Suite 5503, San Francisco, CA 94107, (800) 443-0799

Sierra Club Family Outings, 730 Polk St., San Francisco, CA 94109, (415) 776-2211

The U. S. National Park Service is also a good resource. For more information, call (202) 208-4747 or write to P.O. Box 37127, Washington, DC 20013-7127.

The MATURE TRAVELER

T raveling can be exciting at any time of life, especially for the older person who is in good health. It's not uncommon for older and retired people to begin traveling after saving money for many years. With the excellent medical care and travel opportunities that are available in many foreign countries, there's no reason for mature people to stay at home. Some of the things you'll find in this chapter will stimulate ideas for unique solutions to problems you may have now and in the future.

Group tours are an excellent way for both young and old to travel because all the bothersome details, such as obtaining tickets for events, handling baggage, and arranging hotel reservations are handled by a tour guide. Group travel also offers a way to meet new people, which may lead to new friends, new activities, and even a new career.

Many tours are available through Elderhostel, a Boston based company, which provides entertaining and educational experiences at a low cost. Elderhostel tours are for adults 50 years of age and over, though a companion no younger than 40 may accompany the tour member. Some accommodations are in modern hotel dormitories rather than commercial properties. Elderhostel requires a nonrefundable deposit, but trip cancellation/interruption insurance can be purchased to cover the deposit.

TRAVEL HEALTH TIPS

1. Three to four weeks before you travel, begin a regular exercise program to improve strength, flexibility, and the cardiovascular system.

2. Travel light, and take care of your back. Use curbside check-in at airports.

3. See a physician regularly, and discuss your travel plans, especially if you have chronic conditions or have recently suffered an acute illness.

4. Take important medical information with you.

5. See your ophthalmologist if you have a history of retinal disease, especially if you are flying or going to areas with high altitudes.

6. Get necessary immunization shots ahead of time. Check with your physician to see if you need medication to prevent malaria or if you are going to countries that have strains that are resistant to traditional malaria medications.

7. Take your first aid kit and appropriate labeled medications.

8. Don't forget your Medic-Alert bracelet if you have one.

9. Travelers' assistance insurance for traveling abroad may give you peace of mind.

10. Give yourself a day or two to acclimate when you are going to areas where the climate is different from the climate at home (such as the mountains or the tropics). The key is to get plenty of rest, drink plenty of fluids, and know your own limitations.

11. Proper shoes are a must. It's important to take more than one pair to let the other pair rest or dry out.

12. Take extra medicines with you. Avoid buying medicines abroad. Use caution when taking any medicines for traveler's diarrhea—check with your physician.

13. Organized tours may be less stressful. Additional refer-

ences and specialized tours and trips are listed at the end of this chapter and in the Appendix.

SAFETY AWARENESS FOR THE MATURE TRAVELER

1. Know your own limitations, and be realistic in your expectations. Consider your stamina, walking ability, sleep requirements, rest regulation, and phobias.

2. Travel in groups, especially at night.

3. Protect yourself from robberies, especially in crowds. Pickpockets usually work the metros, subways, and sporting events.

RESOURCES FOR THE MATURE TRAVELER

EdlerTreks is a Canadian tour-operating company that specializes in offbeat destinations. Tours include guides, cooks, and porters; you'll stay in comfortable tourist-class hotels and guest houses with private bathrooms. Travelers sometimes camp outdoors or sleep on air mattresses in a native hut. There may be hiking on nature trails, boat trips, or moderate climbing. Washing facilities may be a communal shower house, a waterfall, or the village pump. Prices include all lodging, support personnel, entrance fees and taxes, land and water transport in the destination country, and most domestic flights. Some meals are included. For a comprehensive brochure including daily itineraries, contact a travel agent or write to **ElderTreks, 597 Markham St., Toronto, Ontario, Canada M6G 2L7.**

AJS Travel Consultants 50+ Club, 177 Beach St., Rockaway Park, New York, NY 11694. Call (800) 221-5002 for brochure on tours and a membership application.

Golden Age Travelers, Pier 27, the Embarcadero, San Francisco, CA 94111, claims more than 9,000 members. This travel group has quarterly travel digests listing tours and cruises. For information call (800) 258-8880.

Golden Tours is a senior travel club that has many kinds of experiences. Contact Golden Tours at (213) 283-7875 or (818) 289-6271.

Seniors Abroad is an international home-stay program for adults over 50. For information, itineraries, and programs for the year, contact Seniors Abroad, 12533 Pacato Circle North, San Diego, CA 92128, (619) 485-1696.

Vagabond Inn Tours and Discounts, 2361 Rosecrans Ave., Ste. 375, El Segundo, CA 90245, (800) 522-1555 for information and reservations.

Books for the Mature Traveler

Elderhostels: The Students' Choice (2nd ed.) by Mildred Hyman (John Muir Publications, 1991), 290 pages, $15.95

Get Up and Go: A Guide for the Mature Traveler by Gene and Adele Malott (Gateway Books, 1989), 325 pages, $10.95

Going Abroad: 101 Tips for Mature Travelers, 347 Congress St., Boston, MA 02210, (800) 248-3737 or (800) 535-8333

The International Health Guide for Senior Citizen Travelers, (516) 422-2225, Pilot Books, 70 pages, 103 Cooper St., Babylon NY 11702, $4.95.

The Mature Traveler, P.O. Box 50820, Reno, NV 89513. Cost for one-year subscription to this newsletter (12 issues) is $24.50. Sample copy $2.00

The 50+ Traveler's Guidebook: Where to Go, Where to Stay, What to Do by Anita Williams and Mary Mac (St. Martin's, 1991), 288 pages, *$12.95*

Unbelievably Good Deals and Great Adventures That You Absolutely Can't Get Unless You're Over Fifty by Joan Rattner Heilman (Contemporary Books, 1990), 261 pages, $7.95

79

TRAVELING with DISABILITIES and MEDICAL CONDITIONS

M any people with physical disabilities and chronic medical conditions (such as asthma or arthritis) fear going to unfamiliar places because of their vulnerability. Recent government regulations have helped people with physical handicaps to travel the globe. These new regulations have led to widespread public acknowledgment of the importance of providing access to cultural events, restrooms, and seating in general to all people, including those with disabilities. If you have a limiting chronic condition, many excellent resources are available to help you stay healthy while you travel. *Don't let a purported handicap keep you from traveling and seeing the world.*

PRE-PLANNING

❖ Do your homework before you leave. There are many excellent resources, including books, newsletters, and informational brochures. Some of them are listed at the end of this chapter and more are in the Appendix.

❖ If you are traveling for the first time, group travel can be an easier way to go. Many travel agents can arrange specialized tours for people with chronic medical conditions or physical disabilities.

❖ Use a wheelchair to and from the airport if you have problems walking or shortness of breath. Don't let a slight restriction in your walking ability keep you from an exciting vacation.

❖ Whether you have a handicap or not, you never know

when you might have to carry your own suitcase, so take as little clothing as possible.

❖ Airline personnel, as well as curbside check-in staff, are usually eager to help you if you ask.

❖ Notify airlines in advance about your disability or condition, and double-check that they have all the pertinent details just prior to flight. If you have the means to travel first class, do so—the personalized attention will be worth it.

❖ It may be important to be a "mechanic" and carry all equipment or tools you need to fix your wheelchair or crutches. A strap may also be helpful in making folding wheelchairs narrow enough to fit through small doorways.

❖ Always carry your important medication with you. Under no circumstances should you pack the medication in your luggage. Luggage is lost under even the most careful circumstances.

❖ Traveling in the spring or fall may be easier because of less crowding and better weather conditions.

❖ Layer the clothing you wear while traveling—it's easier to remove layers as you warm up than to stay warm with insufficient clothing.

❖ If you have a chronic ailment or disability, jet lag may affect you more severely than others. Travel in the daytime as much as possible, get rest before you travel, and avoid alcohol—it can dehydrate you.

❖ If you are a diabetic, a good way to minimize problems while going through customs is to carry a letter from your doctor explaining your need to use syringes. If traveling with a group, tell the group leader and roommates of your condition, and instruct fellow travelers about how to recognize hypoglycemia and what to do should it occur.

81

When traveling to foreign countries, learn how to say, "I have diabetes," or "Sugar or orange juice, please," in the language of the country being visited.

❖ When you take insulin aloft, remember that insulin enters the syringe more easily at high altitudes. And if you cross more than one time zone, ask your physician about adjustments in your insulin schedule. Don't make major changes in your meal plans without first consulting your physician.

❖ The American Heart Association recommends that heart patients carry a copy of a recent electrocardiogram, their physician's business card, a summary of their condition, and a list of necessary medicines (including dose and generic name). In the event of an emergency, the attending physician will be fully informed. If you are visiting an area in a different time zone, especially if only for a few days, keep the medication schedule on your home time.

❖ If your medication needs to be refrigerated, carry a small cooler on a long trip. Ask your pharmacist if you're not sure whether refrigeration is necessary. Bring a note from your physician stating what the medicine is and who it is for.

❖ If you are cruise-bound with medicine that needs refrigeration, take the medicine to the purser's office for refrigeration, or keep it in the ice bucket in your room and alert the cabin steward that you need frequent ice replenishment. When traveling by train, ask the train attendant to be sure to bring you plenty of ice.

❖ Leave all medicine in its original container, especially if you're taking controlled substances such as Tylenol Plus, codeine, or sleeping pills. If you put the medicine in an unlabeled vial, you might be accused of smuggling.

❖ If you need a wheelchair at airports, make your request when you reserve your flight. Ask if you will get door-to-door assistance or if you are responsible for retrieving your own luggage. Arrive at the airport early so you don't miss your flight while waiting for someone to bring the wheelchair. Renew your request for a wheelchair when checking in at the gate to ensure that one will be waiting for you when you land. Finally, try to avoid tight flight connections. You want at least one hour to get from one plane to another.

Important Questions to Ask Tour Providers

1. Is there a handicapped parking area?

2. Is valet parking available?

3. Is a portable ramp available?

4. Do elevator doors open at least 32" wide?

5. Are there special facilities for handicapped guests?

6. It is also important to ask how long the company has been setting up specialized tours.

RESOURCES FOR THE TRAVELER WITH DISABILITIES OR CHRONIC ILLNESS

General Travel: Books and Services

Access Travel, Airport Operations Council, International Consumer Information Center, Department 619-F, Pueblo, CO 81009

Air Travel for the Handicapped, TWA, 605 Third Ave., New York, NY 10158 (212) 290-2121.

Easy Access to National Parks: The Sierra Club Guide for People with Disabilities (also useful for seniors and families with young children) by Wendy Roth and Michael Tompane, (Sierra Club Books, 1992), 404 pages, $16.00

Guide For The Disabled Traveler by Frances Barish (a veteran wheelchair traveler), Frommer-Pasmantier, $10.95, (800) 858-7674.

83

Helping Hands Services for the Handicapped, Greyhound Lines, Section S, Greyhound Tower, Phoenix, AZ 85077

Society for the Advancement of Travel for the Handicapped (SATH), 26 Court Street, Brooklyn, NY 11242, clearinghouse for information about accessible international transportation and lodging facilities

Medic Alert Foundation International, Dept. A2, P.O. Box 1009, Turlock, CA 95381, (800) 344-3226

Travel Ability: A Guide for Physically Disabled Travelers in the United States by Lois Reamy, (Macmillan, 1978) $13.95

Travel for the Disabled: A Handbook of Travel Resources and 500 World Access Guides by Helen Hecker, R.N. (Twin Peaks Press, 1991) 192 pages, $14.95

Travel Industry and Disabled Exchange, 5435 Donna Ave., Tarzana, CA 91356, (818) 343-6339

Traveling Nurses Network, Helen Hecker, R.N., P.O. Box 129, Vancouver, WA 98666, provides specialists, registered nurses for travelers with disabilities (206) 694-2462.

Unique Reservations, 107 13th Ave., Indian Rooks Beach, FL 34635 for patients on kidney dialysis (800) 544-7604

A World of Options for the '90s: A Guide to International Educational Exchange, Community Service and Travel for Persons with Disabilities (Mobility International USA, 1990), 338 pages, $16.00, P.O. Box 3551, Eugene, OR 97403

Handicapped Travelers Association, 121 E. Hillsdale Blvd., Foster City, CA 94404

Handy-Cap Horizons, 3250 E. Loretta Dr., Indianapolis, IN 46220

Information Center for Individuals With Disabilities, Fort Point Place, 27-43 Wormwood St., Boston, MA 02210,(617) 727-5540.

Information Library, National Easter Seal Society for Crippled Children and Adults, 2023 W. Ogden Ave., Chicago, IL 60612

Society for the Advancement of Travel for the Handicapped, 26 Court St., Brooklyn, NY 11242

The Wheelchair Traveler, Ball Hill Rd., Milford, NH 03055

For Diabetics

American Diabetes Association, 11660 Duke Street, Alexandra, VA 23114, offers several helpful items for travelers with diabetes

International Diabetes Foundation (IDF) Directory, IDF, Rue Washington 40, B-1-5. Brussels, Belgium, $35, lists over 100 member associations in over 80 countries

Sugar-Free Sailing, Specialty Cruises, 460 Washington St., Braintree, MA 02184, (800) 228-0558, special cruises for diabetics

Travel and Diabetes Brochure, American Diabetes Association, 600 Fifth Ave., NY 10020, (212) 725-4925

Vacation for Diabetics, (800) 872-8528

Other Medical Conditions

Citizens Emergency Center, (202) 647-5225

Cruises for People With Chronic Lung Disease, Getaway Cruises, Inc., 5 Barnstable Court, Saddle River, NJ 07458, (201) 934-9383

Medic Alert Foundation International, Dept, A2, P.O. Box 1009, Turlock, CA 95381, for travelers with serious diseases, provide metal disks with the medical problem engraved and an emergency telephone number, (800) 344-3226 or (209) 668-3333

Med Escort International, (800) 255-7182

Nursing Escort Services, Cruise Holidays, (619) 484-1000

Passport: A Guide for Traveling Hemophiliacs, National Hemophilia Foundation, 110 Greene St., Suite 406, New York, NY 11012, free to health professionals, 183-page directory that hemophiliacs should carry listing detailed information about services available

Travel for the Patient with Chronic Obstructive Pulmonary Disease, by H. Silver, 1601 18th St,, N.W., Washington, D.C. 20009.

85

Travel Tips for Hearing Impaired People, American Academy of Otolaryngology, 1101 Vermont Avenue, N.W. Suite 302, Washington, D.C. 20005.

Tours for Travelers in Wheelchairs

Accessible Journeys, 35 West Sellers Ave., Ridley Park, PA, (800) 846-4537/(215) 521-0339

Accessible Tours for Directions Unlimited, 720 Bedford Rd., Bedford Hills, NY 10507 (800) 533-5343

Flying Wheels Tours, P.O. Box 382, Owatonna, MN, 55060 (800) 535-6790

Newsletters

The Diabetic Traveler, P.O. Box 8223 RW, Stanford, CT 06905. Send $2.00 for a sample copy, 4 issues/year, $18.95

Handicapped Travel Newsletter, P.O. Box Drawer 269, Athens, TX 75751. Subscription (6-8 issues) $10.00

TRAVELING WHILE PREGNANT

Most physicians agree that you can fly while in the first four to six months of pregnancy if you are experiencing a normal pregnancy. Check with your physician when you are making extensive travel plans. Ask about taking any medication or getting any immunizations. You should address the following points:

1. Country or countries to which you will be traveling

2. Altitude (over 8,000 feet is usually not recommended)

3. Medications you wish to take

4. Immunizations required

OTHER POINTS TO REMEMBER

❖ Choose locations where you can depend on excellent medical care.

❖ When in doubt, avoid areas with potentially hazardous infectious diseases, such as malarial areas.

❖ Some immunizations, such as live virus vaccines, and medications such as tetracyclines, motion sickness medication, and some anti-malarial drugs may be contraindicated with pregnancy.

❖ Choloroquine is a malarial drug considered to be safe for pregnant women. Ask your physician.

❖ Check with your physician about sports activities that are safe for you. Avoid vigorous exercise and activities such as scuba diving or water skiing.

❖ Use special care in hot tubs, saunas, and swimming pools, always bathe afterwards.

❖ When traveling long distances in an automobile, stop frequently and exercise by walking around.

❖ Do not use sunscreens with Paba, as these may cause allergic reactions.

❖ Bring your own vitamin and mineral supplements and medications that you have taken while pregnant to prevent vomiting or diarrhea.

❖ Decreased effectiveness of your immune system may cause significant complications.

The RETURNING TRAVELER

With more people traveling these days, to both heavily populated and remote areas, it's not uncommon for travelers to return home with illnesses. You may find you initially have nonspecific symptoms, such as muscle aches or headaches, before experiencing gastrointestinal or respiratory problems, urinary discomfort, high temperature, or jaundice.

If you do fall ill, see your physician immediately on your return to prevent serious illness. Be ready to answer the following questions:

1. Where did you travel?

2. How long was your stay?

3. What did you eat, drink, or do?

4. What diseases do you believe were prevalent in the area(s) you visited, such as malaria?

5. Is anybody else sick with whom you traveled?

6. Is anybody at home sick who did not travel with you?

7. What immunizations did you receive before your trip?

8. What preventative measures did you take prior to traveling to areas where malaria is prevalent?

Other than taking taking care of any illness, it is not too uncommon to feel a little let down after a wonderful vacation. So it would be a good thing to not only plan your wonderful trip but also to plan something special before you go to look forward to during that first week at home.

IN CONCLUSION...

B efore a final "Bon Voyage," here are a few suggestions for quality renewal time—close to home or abroad.

❖ Spend time with special friends or family for they enrich your life.

❖ Keep active and fit by enjoying your favorite exercise or sport.

❖ Remember you have wonderful things to visit close to home, such as an art museums, an arboretum or just simply window shopping.

❖ Attend a special event, check the entertainment section of your newspaper. You may even develop a new interest by seeing something new.

❖ Spend time at a retreat—plan a weekend away by treating yourself to a deluxe hotel weekend with breakfast in bed.

❖ While traveling, take a good book or magazine to read.

There is a world full of opportunities for renewing the spirit and filling your life with the joy of living. When you plan your time for relaxation, remember to leave the "guilties" at home. You will always have time to take care of those things you have left undone. The important key to healthful travel is careful planning and taking charge of details because peace of mind is your best traveling companion.

APPENDIX

The Appendix is a listing of all kinds of helpful resources for you to refer to as you plan your travels, such as travel insurance companies, gadets to take with you and medical services in the states and abroad.

American consular offices are generally knowledgeable about physicians and hospitals in their service areas. The American Embassy in the capital city of the country you are visiting should also have a 24-hour emergency phone to call for help.

The Superintendent of Documents, U.S. Government Printing Office, Washington, D.C. 20402, also offers information, including leaflets called *Tips for Travelers*, with a separate leaflet for each foreign country. Also available at no charge through the documents office is *Travel Tips for Senior Citizens* and a 32-page booklet, *Your Trip Abroad*, that deals with carrying prescription narcotic drugs. Each publication costs $1.00.

Full-service university teaching hospitals can also be a source of English-speaking physicians and can offer a wide range of medical services. For emergencies in this country or overseas, look for the international symbol for "hospital," a white "H" printed on a blue background.

If you're caught in an medical emergency late at night call the local police. They are most likely to have a list of all-night emergency rooms, drug stores or pharmacies.

In the case of genuine emergency, medical dispensaries at U.S. Armed Forces bases may provide outpatient service to U.S. civilians, but be prepared to prove it's a real emergency.

TRAVEL INSURANCE

In being prepared for an emergency it is wise to be covered by insurance. Check your own medical insurance or travel agency before you leave to find out what coverage they might provide when you travel overseas. Medicare does not cover overseas medical services, although some supplementary policies might. Here is a listing of insurance options:

Access America, P.O. Box 90315 Richmond, VA 23286-4991, 6600 W. Brad St., Richmond, VA 23230, (800) 654-6686 for trip cancellation insurance, for 24-hour hot line (800) 284-8300

American Association of Retired Persons (AARP), 1909 "K" St., N.W. Washington, D.C. 20049. If you are a member, ask about the Medicare Supplement plan for travel

American Express Travel Protection Plan, P.O. Box 919010, San Diego, CA 92191-9010, (800) 234-0375

American Society of Travel Agents, Consumer Affairs Division, 1101 King St., Alexandria, VA 22314, (703) 739-2782, for travel complaints

Carefree Travel Insurance, Box 310, 120 Mineola Blvd., Mineola, Long Island, NY 11501, (516) 294-0220, (800) 645-2424

Europe Assistance International 5670 Wilshire Blvd., Ste. 120, Los Angeles, CA 90036 (travel insurance company), (800) 346-2832. Short-term travel policies, approximately $40.00 for an individual up to eight days of travel and $60.00 for a family

HealthCare Abroad, 219 Investment Bldg., 1511 "K" St., N.W. Washington, D.C. 20005

HealthCare Abroad, Health Care Global, MedHelp Wordwide, 243 Church St., NW, Vienna, VA 22180, (703) 687-3166, (800) 237-6615

International Airline Passengers Association, P.O. Box 870188, Dallas, TX 75287-0188, for baggage protection (800) 527-5888

International SOS Assistance, 1 Neshaminy Interplex, Trevose, PA

19053, Box 11568, Philadelphia, PA, (800) 523-8930 or (215) 244-1500 (in Pennsylvania)

Medical Air Service Association, (800) 643-9023 (for individual membership information on air ambulance services)

Master Assist Medical Protection (Gold MasterCard members only), (214) 994-9843. Referrals for those with medical emergencies who are traveling more than 50 miles from home, 24-hour coverage for services from local doctors, dentists, hospitals and pharmacies.

Mutual of Omaha Teletrip Policy, Box 31762, Omaha, NB 68131, (800) 228-9792

Tel-Trip, (in conjunction with Mutual of Omaha), P. O. Box 31762, Omaha, NB 68131, for trip cancellation insurance (800) 228-9999

Travel Assistance International (a EuropAssistance company), 1333 F St., Washington, D.C. 20004, (202) 331-1609, (800) 821-2828

Travelers Insurance Intl. Company Travel Pak, 52 S. Oakland, East Hartford, CT, 06115, (800) 243-3174 or (203) 528-7663, $25,000 per emergency medical evacuation

Travelguard International, 1145 Clark St., Stevens Point, WI 54481, for trip cancellation insurance (800) 826-1300,

TravMed, P.O. Box 10623, Baltimore, MD 21204, (410) 296-5225, (800) 732-5309

Wallach & Company, Inc. , 107 W. Federal St., P.O. Box 480, Middleburg, VA 22117, (800) 237-6615

World Care Travel Assistance, 1145 Clark St., Steven Point, WI 54481, (800) 253-1877

WorldCare Travel Assistance Association, Inc., 20000 Pennsylvania Ave., N.W., #7600, Washington, D.C. 20006

ACCESSING MEDICAL HELP ABROAD

Global Assist (American Express Card member only), (202)

93

783-7474 (collect from outside the United States) or (800) 554-AMEX (inside U.S.). The operator attempts to set up an appointment with a doctor rather than merely giving the traveler a physician's name and phone number.

VISA Gold (business card holders), (214) 669-8888, toll-free numbers provided for use anywhere in the world. VISA will also set up phone consultations with U.S. doctors.

International Association for Medical Assistance to Travelers (IAMAT), U.S.: 417 Center St., Lewiston, NY 14092. For a free membership card and/or a copy of the directory of participating physicians, call (716) 754-4883 or write to above address for U.S.; Canada: 1287 St. Clair Ave. W., Toronto, M6E 1B8, (416) 652-0137; New Zealand: P.O. Box 5049, Christchurch 5; Switzerland: 57 Voirets, 1212 Grand-Lancy, Geneva. Nonprofit foundation with English-speaking doctors in more than 500 countries who are trained in the United States, Great Britain, or Canada. Great Britain and Canada treat travellers in need of medical care at a set fee schedule for IAMAT members. IAMAT is solely supported by donations from its members. Membership is free, but a $25 membership contribution is appreciated. The 1994 set fee schedule (U.S. currency—subject to change at any time includes office visits: $45.; house, hotel calls: $55.; night calls (9 p.m. to 9 a.m.) Sunday and local holidays: $65. Fees do not apply to physicians called for consult, or for laboratory or surgical procedures, hospitalizations, or any other expenses incurred. IAMAT's responsibilities regarding its physician recommmendations are limited to: review of professional qualifications according to IAMAT standards; physician's ability to speak English or another language in addition to the native tongue; and acceptance of the established IAMAT fee schedule.

International Travelers Hotline at the Center for Disease Control in Atlanta, GA, (404) 332-4559. To receive this document from Superintendent of Documents, U.S. Government Printing

Office, call (202) 783-3238. Refer to publication number CDC 93-8280 (price $6.50)

Overseas Access/EurAide, P.O. Box 2375, Naperville, IL 60567, (708) 420-2343, for more information call (708) 692-6300.

U.S. Access America, 6600 W. Brand St., Richmond, VA 23230, (doctor locator service and special travel insurance), (804) 285-3300. Sells travel insurance with a 24-hour hotline staffed with medical professionals and multi-lingual workers.

U.S. State Department Citizens' Emergency Center, (202) 647-5225, assists Americans who have medical, financial, and legal problems while traveling abroad. Superintendent of Documents, U.S. Government Printing Office, Washington D.C., 20402.

Medical I.D. (Medical Information Service), Health Enterprises, 90 George Levin Dr., Attleboro, MA 02760, (508) 695-0727, (800) MEDIC-ID

You can also find physicians through hotel concierges and American embassies, though all may not be English-speaking doctors.

COMMUNICATION

American Express Traveler's Companion Booklet, (800) 528-4800

AT&T's Language Line, (800) 752-6096

To obtain international calling cards: AT&T—USA Direct, (800) 225-5288; MCI—Call USA: (800) 444-4444; Sprint, (800) 877-4646

Mail Preference Service, Direct Marketing Association, 6 E. 43rd St., New York, NY 10017

U.S. TRAVEL MEDICINE CLINICS

Most of the clinics chosen in this list are associated with medical schools or health departments. They are listed alphabetically by state for your convenience.

95

ALABAMA

Madison County Health Department, 304 Eustis Ave., Huntsville, AL 35801 (205) 539-3711

Travelers' Health Clinic, University of Alabama at Birmingham, Division of Geographic Medicine, 1025 18th St., Rm. 240, Birmingham, AL 35205 (205) 731-9800,

ALASKA

Division of Public Health, 350 Main St., Juneau, AK 99811 (907) 465-3141 or (907) 465-3090,

ARIZONA

Department of Medicine, University of Arizona School of Medicine, 1450 N. Cherry, Tucson, AZ 85719 (602) 626-7900

The Scottsdale Clinic, 9220 E. Mountain View, Scottsdale, AZ 85258 (602) 391-1805

ARKANSAS

Arkansas Department of Health, Communicable Disease Division, 4815 W. Markham, Little Rock, AR 72205-3867 (501) 661-2352

Bentonville Medical Clinic, 306 NE Blake, Bentonville, AR 72712 (501) 273-9056

CALIFORNIA

Department of Health Services, Infectious Disease Branch, Berkeley, CA 94704 (510) 540-2566

Health Care Partners Medical Group of Alhambra, 55 S. Raymond, Ste. 200, Alhambra, CA 91801 (818) 570-8005

Infectious Diseases/Travelers' Clinic, University of California, Davis, Medical Center, Primary Care Center, Ste. C, Sacramento, CA 95817, (916) 734-3741

Scripps Clinic and Research Foundation, Division of Allergy & Immunology, 10666 N. Torrey Pines Rd., La Jolla, CA 92037, (619) 554-8090

Travelers' Clinic & Tropical Diseases Laboratory, University of

96

California, 400 Parnassus St., San Francisco, CA 94143-0560, (415) 476-5787

UCLA Travelers' and Tropical Medicine Clinic, UCLA Medical Center 200 Medical Plaza, # 365, Los Angeles, CA 90024-1688, (310) 206-7663

COLORADO

Colorado Department of Health, 4300 Cherry Creek Dr., South, Denver, CO 80220, (303) 692-2000

Larimer County Health Department, 363 Jefferson St., Ft. Collins, CO 80521, (303) 498-6700

Mesa County Health Department, 515 Patterson Ave., Grand Junction, CO 81501, (303) 244-1743

CONNECTICUT

International Travelers' Medical Service, Division of Infectious Diseases, University of Connecticut Health Center, 263 Farmington Ave., Farmington, CT 06030, (203) 679-4225/(203) 679-3245

Tropical Medicine & International Travelers' Clinic, Yale University School of Medicine, 333 Cedar St., New Haven, CT 06520-8025, (203) 785-2476

DELAWARE

Division of Public Health, P.O. Box 637, Dover, DE 19903, (302) 739-4701

DISTRICT OF COLUMBIA

DC Department of Human Services, 1660 L St., NW, Washington, DC 20009, (202) 673-6738

International Health Service, Georgetown University Medical Center, 3800 Reservoir Rd., NW, Entrance 1, 5th Floor Washington, DC (202) 687-8672

Travelers' Clinic, George Washington University Hospital,

97

Ambulatory Care Center, 22nd & "I" St., Washington, DC 20037, (202) 994-8466

FLORIDA

Travelers' Medical Service, 1411 N. Flagier Dr., Ste. 7900, West Palm Beach, FL 33401, (407) 655-0506

Tropical Medicine & Travelers' Clinic, 3741 Lejeune Rd., SW, Miami, FL 33146-2809, (305) 663-9666

GEORGIA

Georgia Department of Human Resources, 2 Martin Luther King Jr. Dr., 12th Floor, Atlanta, GA 30334, (404) 657-9358

Travel Clinic, University Health Service, University of Georgia, Athens, GA 30602-1755, (706) 542-5575/(706) 542-1162

Travel Well International, Travelers Medical Center, Emory University School of Medicine, Crawford Long Outpatient Center, 20 Linden Ave., Atlanta, GA 30308, (404)686-5885

HAWAII

State Department of Health, P.O. Box 3378, Honolulu, HI 96801, (808) 586-4400

University of Hawaii, Straub Clinic & Hospital, 888 S. King St., Honolulu, HI 96813, (808) 522-4511

IDAHO

Department of Health and Welfare, Main Center for Immunizations, 707 Armstrong Place, Boise, ID 83706, (208) 375-5211, Ext. 231

ILLINOIS

Illinois Department of Public Health, 535 W. Jefferson, Springfield, IL 62761, (217) 785-2060

Travelers' Clinic, University of Chicago Medical Center, University Health Services, 5841 S. Maryland St., Chicago, IL 60637, (312) 702-6840

INDIANA

Fort Wayne-Allen County Health Department, One E. Main St., Fort Wayne, IN 46802, (219) 428-7504

Lake County Health Department, 2293 N. Main St., Crown Point, IN 46307, (219) 738-2020, Ext. 219

IOWA

Immunization Division, State Department of Health, Lucas State Office Bldg., Des Moines, IA 50319, (515) 281-4917

University Hospital, Students Health Service, Iowa City, IA 52242, (319) 335-8370

KANSAS

Montgomery County Medical Health Department, 908 Walnut St., Coffeyville, KS 67337, (316) 251-4210

Watkins Memorial Hospital, Student Health Service, University of Kansas, Lawrence, KS 66045-8830, (913) 864-9500

KENTUCKY

Lexington-Fayette County, Health Department, 650 New Town Pike, Lexington, KY 40508, (606)252-2371

Louisville-Jefferson County Health Department, 400 E. Gray, Louisville, KY 40202, (502) 574-6520

LOUISIANA

Comprehensive Health Clinic, Tulane Medical Center, 1501 Canal St., #505, New Orleans, LA 70112, (504) 588-5199

E. Baton Rouge Parish Health, 353 N. 12th St., Baton Rouge, LA 70821, (504) 342-1788

Louisiana State University, School of Medicine, P.O. Box 33932, Shreveport, LA 71130-3932, (318) 675-5190

MAINE

Department of Human Services, Bureau of Health, State House, Station #11, Augusta, ME 04333, (207) 287-3201

Martin's Point Health Care Center, 331 Veranda St., Portland, ME 04103, (207) 774-5801

MARYLAND

Infectious Diseases/Emporiatics Clinic, Naval Hospital, Bethesda, MD 20899-5011 (301) 295-4237

International Travel Clinic, The Johns Hopkins University, 550 N. Broadway, Rm., 107, Baltimore, MD 21205, (410) 955-8931

Travelers' Health Service, University of Maryland Medical Group, University of Maryland Hospital, 10 S. Pine St., #900, Baltimore, MD 21201, (410) 328-5196

MASSACHUSETTS

Massachusetts Department of Public Health, 150 Tremont St., Boston, MA 02111, (617) 727-7170

Travelers' Advice & Immunization Center, Massachusetts General Hospital, Wang Ambulatory Care Center, 23 Fruit St., Founder's House, Boston, MA 02114, (617) 726-2748

University of Massachusetts Health Service, Amherst, MA (413) 549-2671

MICHIGAN

Interhealth, William Beaumont Hospital, Medical Office Bldg., Ste. 707, 3535 W. Thirteen Mile Rd., Royal Oak, MI 48073, (810) 551-0496

Midwest Travelers' Health Service, Reichert Health Building, Ste. R-4011, Catherine McAuley Health Center, 5333 McAuley Drive, Ypsilanti, MI 48197, (313) 712-2798

MINNESOTA

Airport Medical Clinic, 7775 26th Ave., S., Minneapolis, MN 55450, (612) 726-1771

The Mayo Clinic, Immunization Clinic, Mayo Building, 200 First St., SW, Rochester, MN 55901, (507) 284-8416/(507) 284-2511

MISSOURI

Travelers' Clinic, Family Medicine of St. Louis, Deaconess Medical Office Center, 6125 Clayton Ave., Ste. 201, St. Louis, MO 63139, (314) 768-3685

Washington University School of Medicine, 660 S. Euclid Ave., St. Louis, MO 63110, (314) 362-2998

MONTANA

Montana Department of Health & Environmental Sciences, Cogswell Bldg., Helena, MT 59620, (406) 444-2544

NEBRASKA

Douglas County Health Department, Overseas Clinic, 1819 Farnam St., Omaha, NE 68183, (402) 444-7207

University of Nebraska, Lincoln, Student Health Center, 15th & U Sts., Lincoln, NE 68588, (402) 472-7460

NEVADA

Carson-Tahoe Hospital, P.O. Box 2168, Carson City, NV 89710, (702) 885-4740

International Travel and Immunization Clinic, 1641 E. Flamingo, Ste. 10, Las Vegas, NV 89119, (702) 735-8887

NEW HAMPSHIRE

Dartmouth-Hitchcock Medical Center, Department of Infectious Disease, Travelers' Clinic, 1 Medical Center Dr., Lebanon, NH 03755, (603) 650-5000

New Hampshire Division of Public Health, Health and Welfare Bldg., 6 Hazen Dr., Concord, NH 03301, (603) 271-4551

NEW JERSEY

Isabelle McCosh Infirmary, Princeton University, Princeton, NJ 08544, (609) 258-3129 (yellow fever only)

Rutgers University, Hurtado Health Center, 11 Bishop Pl., New Brunswick, NJ 08903, (908) 932-7401

101

NEW MEXICO

Health and Environmental Department, 1190 St. Francis Dr., Santa Fe, NM 87504, (505) 827-2623

Occupational Medicine and Sports Clinic, Lovelace Medical Center, 5655 Jefferson St., Albuquerque, NM 87108, (505) 343-6300

NEW YORK

Albert Einstein College of Medicine, 1300 Morris Park Ave., Bronx, NY 10461, (718) 430-2059

Columbia Presbyterian Hospital, 630 W. 168th St., New York, NY 10032, (212) 305-2500

Department of Medical and Molecular Parasitology, NY University Medical Center, 550 First Ave., New York, NY 10016, (212) 340-6764

Department of Medicine, Children's Hospital of Buffalo, 239 Bryant St., Buffalo, NY 14222, (716) 878-7751

International Health Care Service, The NY Hospital, Cornell Medical Center, 440 E. 69th St., New York, NY 10021, (212) 472-4284

NORTH CAROLINA

Forsyth County Health Department, Reynolds Health Center, 799 N. Highland Ave., Winston-Salem, NC 27102, (910) 727-8231

International Travel Clinic, Section of Infectious Diseases, Bowman Gray School of Medicine, Wake Forest University, Winston-Salem, NC 27103, (910) 759-5000

Travel Clinic, Duke International, Duke University Medical Center, 1700 Woodstock Rd., Durham, NC 27710, (919) 684-8111

NORTH DAKOTA

Health Promotion and Education, Capitol Bldg., Bismark, ND 58505, (701) 224-2367

OHIO

Case Western Reserve University, Division of Geographic Medicine, Department of Medicine, University Hospital, Cleveland, OH 44106, (216) 368-4818

Ohio Department of Public Health, 246 N. High St., Columbus OH 43216, (614) 466-4626/(614) 466-5404

Ohio University, Hudson Health Center, Athens, OH 45701, (614) 593-1660

OKLAHOMA

Oklahoma Department of Health, NE 10th & Stonewall, Oklahoma City, OK 73152, (405) 271-5601

WorkMed Occupational Health Network, 1923 E. 21st St., Tulsa, OK 74114, (918) 749-5895

OREGON

Benton County Health Department, 530 NW 27th St., Corvallis, OR 97330, (503) 757-6835

Eugene Hospital & Clinic, Immunization Clinic, 1162 Willamette St., Eugene, OR 97401, (503) 687-6041

Portland Occupational Health Center, 3310 NW Yeon Ave., Portland, OR 97210, (503) 227-7562

PENNSYLVANIA

Abington Memorial Hospital, 1235 Old York Rd., #220, Abington, PA 19001, (215) 886-8075

Paoli Memorial Hospital, Occupational Health Department, Medical Office Bldg. 1, Lancaster Ave., Paoli, PA 19301, (215) 648-1430

St. Luke's Hospital, 801 Ostrum St., Bethlehem, PA 18015, (610) 954-4000

RHODE ISLAND

International Health Institute, Brown University, The Miriam Hospital, 164 Summit St., Providence, RI 02906, (401) 274-3700

103

SOUTH CAROLINA

South Carolina Department of Health, Environmental Control, 2600 Bull St., Columbia, SC 29201, (803) 734-5000

SOUTH DAKOTA

State of South Dakota Health Department, 445 E. Capital, Pierre, SD 57501, (605) 773-3737

TENNESSEE

Vanderbilt University Hospital, 21st Ave., South, Nashville, TN 37232, (615) 322-2017

TEXAS

Hermann Hospital, Center for Travel Medicine, 6411 Fannin, Houston, TX 77030, (713) 704-4317

Student Health Center, University of Texas, P.O. Box 7339, Austin, TX 78756 (512) 471-4955

Texas Department of Health, Immunization Section, 1100 W. 49th St., Austin, TX 78756 (512) 458-7405

UTAH

Infectious Disease & HIV Clinic, University of Utah School of Medicine, 50 N. Medical Dr., Salt Lake City, UT 84132 (801) 581-8811

Utah Department of Health, 288 North, 1460 West, Salt Lake City, UT 84116 (801) 538-6101

VERMONT

State Department of Health, 108 Cherry St., Burlington, VT 05401 (802) 863-7323

VIRGINIA

Montgomery County Health Department, 401 Depot St., NW, Christiansburg, VA 24073, (703) 381-7100

Traveler's Clinic, University of Virginia Hospital, Box 485, Health Sciences Center, Charlottesville, VA 22908, (804) 924-9677

WASHINGTON

Auburn Health Center, Seattle-King County Health Department, 20 Auburn Ave., Auburn WA 98002, (206) 833-8400

Bellingham-Whatcom County, Health Department, 1500 N. State St., Bellingham, WA 98227, (206) 676-4593

Travel & Tropical Medicine Clinic, University of Washington, School of Medicine, 1959 NE Pacific St., RC-02, Seattle, WA 98195, (206) 548-4226, (206) 548-4888

Travelers' Medical & Immunization Clinic of Seattle, 509 Olive Way, Ste., 1201, Seattle, WA 98101, (206) 624-6933

WEST VIRGINIA

Travelers' Clinic, Marshall University School of Medicine, 1801 Sixth Ave., Huntington, WV 25703, (304) 696-7046, (304) 525-0275

WISCONSIN

International Travelers' Clinic, St. Luke's Medical Center, 2900 W. Oklahoma Ave., Milwaukee, WI 53215, (414) 649-6664/6666

University of Wisconsin, Madison Health Service, 1552 University Ave., Madison WI 53705, (608) 262-1388

U.S. COMPANIES THAT PROVIDE AIR AMBULANCE SERVICE

AirAmbulance Network, Miami, FL, (305) 447-0458, (800) 327-1966)

International SOS, Box 11568, Philadelphia, PA 19116, (215) 244-1500, (800) 523-8930

Life Flight, Hermann Hospital, Houston, Texas, (800) 2311-4357

National Jets, Fort Lauderdale, FL, (305) 359-9900, (800) 327-3710

Nationwide/Worldside Emergency Ambulance Return (NEAR), 450 Prairie Ave., Calument City, IL 60409, (800) 654-6700

EQUIPMENT FOR HEALTHY TRAVEL

Acclimator, The Jet Lag Watch, (800) 7-JET-LAG

AccuFilter 5 Water Purifying Straw is filled with filtering membranes that catch organisms. $21.95. Global Star Productions, 10101 So. Western Oklahoma City, OK 73139, (416) 470-7460; Fax: (416) 470-7499

AIDS Prevention Kits, Safeco Manufacturing Ltd., 947 Warden Ave., Toronto, Ontario M1L 4E3, (416) 752-6740, contains needles, sutures, intravenous supplies, and other materials for emergency care.

American Red Cross First Aid Kit, available from Red Cross chapters, $19.95

Antibacterial Toothbrush Compact Designs of New York makes Hygeia, a toothbrush made of bristles that neutralize the germs that can build up in normal toothbrushes, $5.95

Aqua Pill Timer, Zeko Industries, (800) 431-2486, an electronic timer to remind you to take your medicines; includes water and built-in straw

CADD-TPN: Ambulatory Infusion Systems, Pharmacia Deltiec, Inc., St. Paul, MN 55112, (800) 426-2448, portable parental nutrition system

Chinook Medical Gear, Inc., 2805 Wilderness Place, Suite 700, Boulder, CO 80301, (800) 766-1365

DEET, Impregnated ankle and wrist bands to keep mosquitos at bay, effective for 120 hours. Two-pair pack $19.95. Florida Caribbean Manufacturer, 21925 U.S. Highway 19 North, Clearwater, FL 34625, (813) 726-7798 (813) 726-7164

EcoWater is a countertop distiller that boils water to 212 degrees Fahrenheit, converts it to steam, and then condenses it into purified water, 120-volt model, $105.99 plus state sales tax; 230-volt model, $125.99 plus state state sales tax, P.O. Box 64420, St. Paul, MN 55164 (800) 86-WATER.

Expedition Medical Kit, for expeditions to remote areas with supplies designed for use by large groups to stop major bleeding, treat dehydration, and manage dental emergencies. A sampling of supplies in the kit includes trauma pads, dressings, bandages, splinter removal forceps, antibacterials, Pepto-Bismol, and a first-aid book. $129.95. The **Traveler's Medical Kit,** a smaller version, is designed for use by groups of one to four people; $89.95.

Ident-A-Tot, 7216 Mandan Rd. Greenbelt, MD, (301) 345-7029, Identification system for kids, ideal for large amusement parks and crowded airports.

LensCard, the size of a credit card, contains a tiny piece of microfilm on one side and a dime-sized magnifying lens on the other. When you bend the card in the middle, the lens magnifies the medical information. LensCard can hold up to one printed page, with such information as special medical conditions, blood type, emergency contacts, and physicians' and hospitals' names. $11.95. Available from LensCard Systems, (800) 322-3025 (answering machine).

MEDI-UNIT, for people in need of supplementary oxygen, medical supply stores sell portable tanks. In Alhambra, California, a store sells portable tanks with a case and shoulder strap or with a cart for $220.00-$275.00. MEDI-UNIT, (818) 281-2103 (answering machine), or medical supply stores. **Airline policies regarding use of oxygen vary; some airlines provide it for a fee.**

Noise for Sleeping, Hammacher Schlemmer, New York, (800) 543-3366, (ask for catalog), gadgets reproduce sound of surf, rain, or other "pleasant environmental sounds," provides background noise, prices vary. Ops. Center, 9180 LE Saint Dr., Fairfield, OH 45014.

PentaPure Travel Cup: Another water purifier which treats small quantities of water quickly. $29.95.

PUR Traveler: To reduce the danger of contamination through drinking water in foreign countries, can purify 400 quarts on one filter cartridge. $69.95, (800) 845-7873

Soother Companion: To avoid sleepless nights and quell noisy hotel environs, there is a travel-size white-noise generator that emits a mixture of sound waves to mask noise. The machine is about the size of a hardcover book. $99.95. Sharper Image, (800) 344-4444.

Spider Portable Mosquito Net, Thai Occidental LTD., 5334 Yonge St., Suite 907, Toronto, Canada M2N 6M2, (416) 498-4277, $69.95 (Canadian) plus shipping and handling, suspends from the ceiling and gives large pest-free area for sleeping or working

Swiss Army Knife Compact Emergency Kit fits in a leather pouch about 4 inches square. Contains 19 items. SOS Kit, $135.00. Travel-Smith, (800) 950-1600, FAX: (416) 496-3490, 2935 Kerner Blvd., San Rafael, CA 94901

Tick Tongs, GM Trading, Box 234, Saddle River, NJ 07458-0234, $4.95 plus $1.35 for handling, pressure applying paddle-shaped "locking tongs" designed for grasping embedded ticks at the skin line

Toilet Seat Cover, Camphor Camping Supplies, 810 Route 17 North Paramus, NJ 07653-0997, (800) 526-4784, sanitary, disposable seat covers

Traveling Tote Bag, World Trade Center, 24310-M Moulton Pkwy., Laguna Hills, CA 92651. This store has the most complete section of travel accessories west of Chicago.

Wonder Roll Self-Inflating Automatic Adjustment Back Support, To avoid aching backs on long trips, from GNR Health Systems, (800) 523-0912, $29.95

World Status Map, Box 466, Merrifield, VA 22116, (703) 564-8473, published monthly, $36 per year, lists all countries that have civil disorders, border conflicts, disease outbreaks, other hazards, and other unusual situations.

RECOMMENDED READING

Newsletters

Travel newsletters can be a valuable source of information, and their numbers continue to grow. There are 192 travel newsletters now distributed throughout North America. In 1991 there were 140 and in 1992 they increased to 187. Newsletters cover countries as different as Mexico and Germany, and include topics like gay travel and railroads.

Most newsletters are 8 1/2 x 11 inches and tend to use graphics and line drawings. The most serious are long on phone numbers, addresses and prices and relatively short on colorful descriptions.

Several newsletters accept no underwriting or freebies from the hotels, restaurants and transportation-providers they write about, but others frequently accept free and specially discounted service. Their publications may still include valuable information, but travelers should keep possible built-in biases in mind.

The best place for a reader to browse among titles and get further information is the *Oxbridge Directory of Newsletters*, which is available in the reference department of most large public libraries.

Consumer Reports Travel Letter, P.O. Box 53629, Boulder, CO 80322, (800) 234-1970, is the foremost travel newsletter in the country, carefully appraising bargain opportunities and freely criticizing major players, concentrating more on ways and means than on specific destinations.

Inside Flyer, 4715-C Town Center Dr., Colorado Springs, CO 80916, (719) 597-8889, is considered the "bible" of newsletters for the fanatically frequent flyer. Explaining how to exploit frequent-traveler offerings of the airlines, hotels and rental car companies, this publication accepts advertising, but is known for editorial independence and provides no coverage of destinations.

Accessible Journeys, 412 South 45th St., Philadelphia, PA 19104, travel information, a newsletter, and tours for the disabled.

109

The Affluent Gourmet Traveler, Healthy Gourmet, Inc., Gourmet Bldg., P. O. Box 102, Middle Island, NY 11953-0102, (516) 924-8555, published monthly, $48 per year, focuses on the affluent gourmet traveler desiring delicious, healthy worldwide culinary excellence and entertainment.

Agent's Cruise Monthly, World Ocean & Cruise Liner Society, P.O. Box 92, Stamford, CT 06904, (203) 329-2787, published monthly, $60 per year, provides cruise information for travel agents.

Aha, Alfred Eichner, 1408 Baritone Court, Vienna, VA 22180, (703) 938-1890, contains brainteasers, puzzles, and games.

Britainews, (also known as "Britain Travel News") British Tourist Authority, 40 West 56th St., Suite 320, New York, NY 10019, published quarterly, promotes tourism in Britain, publicizes industrial and trade fairs, and provides current information on tours, accommodations and transportation.

Bulletin Voyages, Les Editions Acra Limitee, 78 Blvd., St. Joseph West, Canada H2T 2PY, (514) 287-9773, published weekly, $50 per year, carries information on programs offered by tour operators and transportation companies, as well as articles on destinations, written in French.

Business Travel News, CMP Publications, Inc., 600 Community Dr., Manhasset, NY 11030, (516) 562-5000, published biweekly, provides information on hotel and rental car industries, airline competition in Europe, and other corporate travel matters.

The Business Traveler, Maritz Travel Company, 1395 North Highway Dr., Fenton, MO 63099, (314) 827-4000, covers air travel issues, including frequent flying, airplane safety, airport shopping, airport security, group airfares, children flying solo, and air traffic control.

The Diabetic Traveler, P.O. Box 8223, Stamford, CT 06905, published quarterly, $18.95 per year, newsletter for the traveler with diabetes, including useful tips and destinations with the diabetic in mind

110

Family Travel Times, Travel With Your Children, 45 W. 18th St., New York, NY 10011, (212) 206-0688, $35 per year, offers many up-to-date listings and ideas for family vacations.

FitNews, AR&FA, 9310 Old Georgetown Rd., Bethesda, MD 20814, $25 per year

Guide to Traveling with Arthritis, Box 307-G, Coventry, CT 06238, free brochure published by Upjohn

The Harvard Health Letter, P.O. Box 420300, Palm Coast, FL 32142-0300. For free sample copy, send request to 164 Longwood Ave., Dept. LA, P.O. Box 380, Boston, MA 02117

Immunization Alert, Kenneth Dardick, M.D., P.O. Box 406, Storrs, CT 06268, (203) 487-0422, computer printouts of immunizations, preventative medications, and other useful health information

International Living, (301) 234-0515, $48 per year, features articles about international travel, lifestyles, investments, retirement and employment, including monthly currency reports.

International Travel Warning Service, WSM Publishing Company, P.O. Box 466, Merrifield, VA 22116, (703) 525-3502, published monthly, contains danger and disease warnings for international travelers, including passport, visa, and vaccination requirements for all countries.

International Visitor, International Visitor Publishing, Inc., 799 Broadway, NY 10003, (212) 533-9405, 10 issues per year, $78.50 per year, acts as clearinghouse of information to help U.S. travel industry "attract international visitors, profit from their spending, and enhance their experiences."

Jet Lag Diet, Argonne National Laboratories, Dept. BH, 9700 South Cass, Argonne, IL 60439, send a self-addressed, stamped envelope for a free brief discussion on jet lag diets.

The Mature Traveler, GEM Publishing Group, P.O. Box 50820, Reno, NV 89513, (702) 786-7419, published monthly, $24.50 per year, provides information and advice to help older Americans in their travel and vacation plans.

The Rep Travel Newsletter, United Association of Manufacturers' Representatives (UAMR), 133 Terrace Trail W., Lake Quivira, KS 66106, published monthly, provides business and vacation travel tips for manufacturers' representatives, including information on tours and travel discounts

Romantic Traveling, Winterbourne Press, 236 West Portal Ave., Suite 237, San Francisco, CA 94127, FAX: (415) 731-8239, published quarterly, $15 per year, focuses on travel to "romantic spots throughout the world."

Runzheimer Reports on Travel Management, Runzheimer and Company, Inc., 555 Skokie Blvd., Suite 340, Northbrook, IL 60062, (708) 291-9011, published monthly, $295 per year, covers travel budgets, corporate arrangements with travel agencies, in-house travel departments, and travel policies for business firms.

SporTreks, Symmetry Publishing, Box 623, Lebanon, NH 03766, $36 per year, monthly newsletter for travelers who take fitness-consciousness seriously.

Travel Medicine Advisor, American Health Consultants, P.O. Box 740056, Atlanta, GA 30374, (800) 688-2421 or (404) 262-7436.

The Travelin' Talk Newsletter, Travelin Talk, P.O. Box 3534, Clarksville, TN 37043-3534, (615) 552-6670, published quarterly, serves as an update on available trips, tours, and other activities for the information network.

Traveling Healthy, Traveling Healthy, Inc., 108-48-70th Rd., Forest Hills, NY 11375, (718) 268-7290, published bimonthly, $24 per year, discusses health and medical issues of interest to travelers.

Traveling Healthy and Comfortably, 108-48 - 70th Rd., Forest Hills, NY 11375. Bi-monthly, $32.00, sample issue $4.00.

The Upjohn Jet Lag Booklet, Box Z307, Coventry, CT 06238.

The Wellness Newsletter, 3451 Central Avenue, St. Petersburg, FL 33713.

112

Wilderness Medical Society, P.O. Box 397, Point Reyes, CA 94956, scholarly journal and newsletter for physicians and others interested in health problems of the outdoors

The Wellness Letter, 48 Shattuck Sq., Suite 43, Berkeley, CA 94704, bi-monthly, $30.00

Wilderness Medicine Newsletter, Wilderness Medicine Newsletter, P.O. Box 9, Pitkin, CO 81241, published six times per year, $20

The World Weather Guide, (800) 773-3000.

TRAVEL BOOKS

The Business Travel Survival Guide by Jack Cummings (John Wiley & Sons), 396 pages, $14.95

Foreign Travel and Immunization Guide by Hans H. Neumann (Medical Economics Book, 1987) 96 pages $24.95

Health Guide for International Travelers by Thomas P. Sakmar, Pierce Gardner, M.D., and Gene Peterson, M.D. (Passport Books, 1993), 160 pages, $5.95

Health Information for International Travel (U.S. Department of Health and Human Services, 1993), 180 pages, $6.00

International Travel Health Guide, by Stuart R. Rose, M.D. (Travel Medicine, Inc., 1992), 400 pages, $17.95. Updated yearly using the latest data from the World Health Organization, U.S. Centers for Disease Control and travel medicine experts worldwide. Includes topics such as country-by-country disease risks, vaccinations, listings of doctors and hospitals—used extensively and recommended by physicians, corporations, and travel agencies.

Overcoming Jet Lag by Charles F. Ehret and Lynn Waller Scanlon (Berkeley Books, 1993), 160 pages, $7.95

The Safe Travel Book: A Guide for the International Traveler by Rev. Peter Savage (Free Press, 1993), 128 pages, $12.95

Staying Healthy in Asia, Africa, and Latin America: Your Complete

Health Guide to Traveling and Living in Less-Developed Regions of the World by Dirk Schroeder (Volunteers in Asia Press, 1993), 185 pages, $10.95

Travel and Learn, The New Guide to Educational Travel (2nd ed.) by Evelyn Kaye (Blue Penguin Publications, 1992), 346 pages, $23.95

The Travel and Tropical Medicine Manual by Elaine C. Jong, M.D. (W. B. Saunders, 1987), 352 pages, $25.95

The Traveler's Guide to Homeopathy by Phyllis Speight (C. W. Daniel Co.), 72 pages, $12.95

The Traveler's Handbook edited by Melissa Shales (Globe Pequot Press, 1988), 820 pages, $8.95

Travelers' Medical Resource, by William W. Forgey, M.D. 875 pages, $19.95. Detailed medical information on 219 countries and a first aid manual for when you get there.

Traveler's Self Care Manual by William F. Forgey, M.D. (ICS Books, 1990), 128 pages, $6.95.

Traveling Healthy by Sheila H. Hillman and Robert Hillman, M.D. (Penguin Books, 1980).

The Year-Round Traveler's Health Guide by Patrick Doyle, M.D. and James E. Banta, M.D. (Acropolis Books)

Your Medicine Chest: A Consumer's Guide to the Effects of Prescription and Non-Prescription Drugs by Wayne O. Evans, Ph.D., and Jonathan O. Cole, M.D. (Little Brown, 1990), 128 pages, $6.95.

POCKET GUIDES

A Comprehensive Guide to Wilderness and Travel Medicine, by Eric Weiss, M.D., 106 pages, $4.95, included in most Adventure Medical Kits. Invaluable reference covers not only the basics of first aid, but a comprehensive list of wilderness medical topics.

Mountain Sickness: Prevention, Recognition and Treatment, by Peter H. Hackett, M.D. (American Alpine Club, 1991), 71 pages, $6.50.

Mountaineering Medicine: A Wilderness Medical Guide, by Fred T. Darvill, Jr., M.D. (Wilderness Press, 1992), 102 pages, $4.95. An excellent pocket-size handbook of mountaineering medicine.

The Pocket Doctor: Your Ticket to Good Health While Traveling, by Stephen Bezruchka, M.D. (The Mountaineers, 1992), 84 pages, $4.95. Pocket-size handbook features clear, concise information on everything from common complaints to life-threatening emergencies.

Travelers' Medical Alert: China, by William W. Forgey, M.D. (ICS Books, 1991), 125 pages, $6.99. Medical information for traveling Americans and Canadians.

Travelers' Medical Alert: Mexico, by William W. Forgey, M.D. 144 pages, $6.99.

Travelers' Self-Care Manual, by William W. Forgey, M.D., 128 pages, $6.95. Simple, practical aid for international travelers.

OUTDOOR, WILDERNESS & SURVIVAL BOOKS

A Medical Guide to Hazardous Marine Life by Paul S. Auerbach, M.D. (Mosby Yearbook, 1991), 64 pages $17.95. Medical guide for scuba divers and others who explore the unique marine environment.

Accidents in North American Mountaineering, 1992 compiled and published by The American Alpine Club and The Alpine Club of Canada, 66 pages, $7.00. Descriptions and analyses of mountaineering accidents.

Backpacking with Babies and Small Children by Goldie Silverman (Wilderness Press/Berkeley Books, 1986), 144 pages, $9.95

Bear Attacks: Their Causes and Avoidance by Stephen Herrero. (Lyons and Burford, 1988), 292 pages, $12.95. Interesting and instructive reading for those who go into bear country.

Emergency Survival Handbook (American Outdoor Safety League), 45 pages, $3.50. Indexed, pocket-sized guide to successfully dealing with medical and outdoor emergencies.

115

Going Higher: The Story of Man and Altitude by Charles S. Houston, M.D. (Little, 1987), 300 pages, $12.95. Comprehensive and explicit layperson's reference on the history of high altitude effects, illnesses and treatments.

High Altitude: Illness and Wellness by Charles Houston, M.D. (ICS Books, 1993), 80 pages, $6.99. All about mountain sickness with many case histories.

Hypothermia, Frostbite and Other Cold Injuries by James A. Wilkerson, M.D., editor; Cameron C. Bangs, M.D., John S. Hayward, Ph.D. (The Mountaineers), 101 pages, $11.95. Very important reference if you are going to cold environments.

Medicine for Mountaineering edited by James A. Wilkerson, M.D., 350 pages, $16.95, considered the "Bible" of mountaineering medicine.

Medicine for the Backcountry by Buck Tilton and Frank Hubbell. (ICS Books, 1990), 192 pages, $9.95. Comprehensive and clearly written handbook ... highly illustrated.

Medicine for the Outdoors by Paul S. Auerbach, M.D. (Little, 1986), 348 pages, $12.95; illustrated, $24.95) Medical text for all backcountry emergencies and ailments.

Medicinal Wild Plants by Bradford Angier (Stackpole, 1978), 320 pages, $16.95. Complete information for identifying over a hundred native North American plants and their traditional uses.

MedDive by Kathy Work, R.N., and contributing author Jon Kushner, (Dive Rescue, 1991), 123 pages, $19.95. A technical manual for rescue teams and dive professionals.

NOLS Wilderness First Aid by Tod Schimelpfenig and Linda Lindsey. (Stackpole, 1992), 368 pages, $12.95. Includes all fundamental topics, and first aid kits for wilderness use.

The Outward Bound Wilderness First Aid Handbook by Peter Goth, M.D., and Jeffrey Isaac, (Lyons and Burford, 1991), $13.95,

116

comprehensive guide covers what you need to know to treat injuries and illnesses in a wilderness setting.

Wilderness Search & Rescue by Tim J. Setnicka (AMC Books, 1980), 656 pages, $29.95. For trip leaders or professionals entrusted with lives in the outdoors... covers all aspects of search and rescue.

Ticks by Roger Drummond, Ph.D. (Wilderness Publishing, 1990), 60 pages, $4.95.) Describes all common ticks, the diseases they carry, symptoms and treatments.

Waterlover's Guide to Marine Medicine by Paul G. Gill (S & S Trade, 1993), 192 pages, $12.00. Provides emergency treatments as well as followup protocol.

VIDEOTAPES

Medicine for the Outdoors, by Paul S. Auerbach, M.D., 50 minutes, $17.95. Up-to-date first aid video

The Very Healthy Traveler, by Caroline L. MacLeod, M.D., 29 minutes, $24.95. Covers an impressive range of travel health-related topics.

MISCELLANEOUS RESOURCES

The ACCESS Foundation for the Disabled, P.O. Box 356, Malverne, NY 11565, (516) 568-2715

The Invented City, 41 Sutter St., Suite 1090, San Francisco, CA 94104, (800) 788-2489 in U.S., (415) 673-0347 worldwide

Vacation Exchange Club, P.O. Box 820, Haleiwa, HI 96712, (800) 638-3841

Worldhomes Holiday Exchange, 1707 Platt Crescent N., Vancouver, BC V7J 1X9, Canada, (604) 987-3262

Academic Travel Abroad, 3210 Grace St. N.W., Washington, D.C. 20007, (202) 333-3355

117

American Automobile Association (call the office in your city), warnings about high-crime areas in North America

The Adventure Vacations Catalog (Simon & Schuster), $14.95

Dialysis In Wonderland (a vacation program for travelers and vacationers who require kidney dialysis), Building 535, University of Utah, Salt Lake City, UT 94112, (801) 581-8566

Don't Drink The Water by Stanley Seah and *Things Your Travel Agent Never Told You* by Gordon Stuart. (Grovenor House/Canadian Health Association, $6.95 each.

Medical Guide for the International Traveler, Immunization Center, 18411 Clark St., Tarzana, CA 91356, $1.00

Maupintour Tours P.O. Box 807, Lawrence, Kansas, 66044 (800) 255-4266 provides cancellation insurance.

The Sophisticated Traveler/11 Cities Of Europe, personal observations of 30 writers (Villard Books), $14.95

Pet Passport by Ronald and Michelle DeGroot, P.O. Box 10223, Beverly Hills, CA 90213, (310) 202-8255

Pet Transportation (travel agency for pets), 3382 University Ave., San Diego, CA 92104, (714) 281-4800

Trading Places: The Wonderful World of Vacation Home Exchanging by Bill and Mary Barbour (Rutledge Hill Press, 1991), 192 pages, $9.95

The Vacation Home and Hospitality Exchange Guide by John Kimbrough (Kimco Communications, 1991), 175 pages, $14.95

Working Holidays, Canadian Bureau for International Education, 141 Lawyer Ave., West Ottawa, Ontario K1P 5J3, Canada, $10.95

FOREIGN LANGUAGE MEDICAL PHRASES
FRENCH

"Je suis malade. Emmmenz-moi a l'hôspital immediament."
"I'm sick. Take me to a hospital."

"J'ai mal ici_____." **(Ondoquez où)**
"I have pain here_____." (Indicate where)

"Où sont les toilettes?"
"Where are the toilets?"

"J'ai la diarrhée."
"I have diarrhea."

"J'ai du diabète"
"I have diabetes."

"J'ai de l'asthme."
"I have asthma."

"J'ai un problems cardiaque."
"I have a heart (cardiac) problem."

"J'ai une allergie a_____." **(Indiquer a quoi)**
"I have an allergy to_____." (Indicate to what)

"Je ne parle pas votre langue."
"I do not speak your language."

GERMAN

"Ich bin krank. Bitte bringen sie mich sofort ins."
"I'm sick. Take me to a hospital."

"Ich habe schmerzen... hier_____." **(Auf die betreffends)**
"I have pain here_____." (Indicate where)

"Wo ist die toilette?"
"Where is the toilet?"

"Ich habe durchfall."
"I have diarrhea."

"Ich bin zuckerkrank."
"I have diabetes."

"Ich habe asthma."
"I have asthma."

"Ich bin herzkrank."
"I have a heart (cardiac) problem."

"Ich bin allergisch gegen_____." **(Allergie angeben)**
"I have an allergy to_____." (Indicate to what)

119

"Ich spreche ihre Sprache nicht."
"I do not speak your language."

SPANISH

"Me siento mal. Lléveme al hospital immediatamente."
"I'm sick. Take me to a hospital."

"Me duele aqui_____." (Indique dónde)
"I have pain here_____." (Indicate where)

"¿Dónde están los servicios?"
"Where are the toilets?"

"Tengo diarrea."
"I have diarrhea."

"Tengo asma."
"I have asthma."

"Tengo un problema de corazón/un problem cardiaco."
"I have a heart (cardiac) problem."

"Soy alérgico/a a_____." (Indique a qué)
"I have an allergy to_____." (Indicate to what)

"No hablo su idioma."
"I do not speak your language."

ITALIAN

"Sono malato/a. Mi porti all'ospedale immediatamente."
"I'm sick. Take me to a hospital."

"Mi fa male qui_____." (Indica dove)
"I have pain here_____." (Indicate where)

"Ho la diarrea."
"I have diarrhea"

"Ho il diabete."
"I have diabetes."

"Ho l'asma."
"I have asthma."

"Sono malato/a du cuore (Ho problemi cardiaci)."
"I have a heart (cardiac) problem."

"Sono allergico/a a_____." (Indica a che cosa).
"I have an allergy to_____."(Indicate to what)

"Non parlo la sua lingua."
"I don't speak your language."

SWAHILI

"Mimi nimgonjwa nipeleke hospitali maramoja."
"I'm sick. Take me to a hospital."

"Nina maumivu hapa_____." (Sema wapi)
"I have pain here_____." (Indicate where)

"Choo kiko wapi?"
"Where are the toilets?"

"Ninahara."
"I have diarrhea."

"Nina ugonjwa wa sukari."
"I have diabetes."

"Nina ugonjwa wa pumu."
"I have asthma."

"Nina ugonjwa wa moyo
"I have a heart (cardiac) problem."

"Kudhuru_____." (Sema kwanini)
"I have an allergy to_____." (Indicate to what)

"Sisemi lugha yenu."
"I don't speak your language."

IMPORTANT TELEPHONE ADDRESSES & NUMBERS

_____

_____

_____

_____

_____

_____

_____

_____

_____

_____

_____

_____

_____

_____

_____

_____

_____

_____

_____

_____

_____

_____

_____

_____

_____